Darrell,

Best Wishes!!

You're
HIRED

You're
HIRED

HOW TO
SUCCEED IN
BUSINESS
AND LIFE

From the Winner of
THE APPRENTICE

BILL RANCIC

with Daniel Paisner

HarperBusiness

An Imprint of HarperCollinsPublishers

HarperCollins books may be purchased for educational, business, or sales promotional use. For information please write: Special Markets Department, HarperCollins Publishers Inc., 10 East 53rd Street, New York, NY 10022.

Designed by Timothy Shaner

Photo Insert Design by William Ruoto

Library of Congress Cataloging-in-Publication Data has been filed for.

ISBN 0-06-076541-0

09 10 11 DIX/RRD 10 9 8 7

For my dad, who I know is watching down over me

Money is better than poverty,
if only for financial reasons.

–WOODY ALLEN

CONTENTS

TRUMP
THE TRUMP ORGANIZATION

The Apprentice has been a great deal of fun for me—and at the same time a learning experience. Yes, I've built landmark buildings and timeless golf courses. I've made some wonderful business deals and dueled with some of the wiliest competitors. But in the end, running a great business is about hiring great people and putting them in the right jobs.

So when the opportunity came to run a national job search—with 215,000 applicants—I was excited from the start. Surrounding yourself with smart, ambitious folks makes all the difference to an executive. And the art of hiring is one of the most important parts of any large and successful business, and the least understood. *The Apprentice* gave me—and the world—a chance to see what separates a good candidate from a great employee. I didn't know what to expect from the talented pool of young businessmen and -women who made it to the final competition. What I did know was that I needed a support team I could trust and rely on. So during the show I was looking at every candidate to see those special attributes that would make them a valuable addition to The Trump Organization.

I was looking for someone I could leave in charge of a multimillion-dollar project, who could make decisions but also follow instructions, who had a proven mastery of the fundamentals of business but who could also adapt and improvise. I wanted someone with leadership abilities, charisma, and moral fiber, and most important, someone who could be both a teacher and a student—an asset essential for any kind of team captain.

I had my eye on Bill Rancic from the beginning. He reminded me of myself at a young age. He was hungry, worked well with his partners, and brought a different and unique set of skills to each task he was given.

In the end, he proved he has what it takes to win the show. But his path to success didn't just start with his audition tape. Before he came to New York, he'd already had numerous successes in business. You might say that he'd earned the equivalent of an MBA through his own ingenuity and hard work. That's what I look for when I'm building a winning team, people who bring a different set of eyes and skills to the business to keep things fresh and moving forward, and that's why I said, "You're hired!" to Bill Rancic.

Now he's written a book that uses his own unique experiences to help the average armchair businessperson succeed as well, and the techniques he offers can be applied to anyone from a seventh grade whiz kid to a corporate CEO. He's my apprentice for a reason, so listen up and maybe I'll see you in the boardroom one day too.

Donald Trump

INTRODUCTION
Why We're Here

> Being good in business is the most fascinating kind of art. Making money is art and working is art and good business is the best art.
>
> —Andy Warhol

L et's get one thing straight right from the start. Ever since I walked away with the top prize on the NBC reality show *The Apprentice*, starring Donald Trump—a job running a division of The Trump Organization, at a starting salary of $250,000—I've been on the receiving end of a rush of public attention that has shone a weird (and sometimes harsh) spotlight on everything I've done, everything I'm doing, and everything I might do next.

Okay, so I might have suspected as much going in, but I didn't think things through. Why? Well, I wasn't conditioned to think about things like celebrity and publicity and people asking for an autograph while you're hurrying to catch a plane. I thought about the opportunities the show would offer, the chance to work alongside Donald Trump and to test my business instincts against some of the best and brightest young entrepreneurs the producers could find, but I didn't think about any fame or fortune that might come my way as a result. That wasn't what it was all about—at least not for me. There were sixteen of us on the show to start, and we've all had to deal with our own take on this celebrity business now that we've been returned to the rest of our lives, but all I can do is speak for myself. From where I sit, I don't know that I'll ever get used to all the noise.

That said, I like to think all this noise is actually *about* something, that there's something to all the attention beyond hype. I happen to believe that one of the reasons *The Apprentice* struck such a chord was that it spoke to some of the core values that define us all. It was all about hard work and dedication, striving to succeed, which worked out nicely for me because I was about those things as well. Anyway, that's how I approached my own career. I accomplished a whole lot in that career, in a relatively short stretch of time, long before the concept for *The Apprentice* was ever kicked around in a pitch meeting, and I'm not done yet, but the success of the show and my success on it have presented me with a new set of options and opportunities. Take this book. I mean, here I am writing a book on business strategies for young entrepreneurs, and there you are on the receiving end of the notion. At the very least, you've gotten past the book jacket and the display in the store to check out these opening remarks, so there's something going on here, some new equation at work, some pop-culture bargain we are now positioned to make with each other. Strange, isn't it? A year ago, I wouldn't have even considered setting my thoughts down on paper and writing a book, and if I had, chances are you would never have considered buying it—even though I had the same things to say back then as I do now and presumably you had the same desire to learn some new approaches.

So what gives? What's changed? Well, I don't know that anything's changed except that now I've got a microphone and a camera pointed at my face and folks seem to look at me as some kind of hardworking, hard-charging, hard-to-pigeonhole young businessman who appears headed in the right direction. That's pretty much where it begins and ends, if you ask me. The clock will run out on my fifteen minutes of fame, I can be sure of that, and I'll go back to working my butt off, hustling to get and keep a leg up in a competitive corporate environment, putting to work some of the lessons I learned at the feet of one of the world's boldest entrepreneurs, reaching for my own version of the American dream and hoping to outreach the person next to me.

> **M**ake your vocation your vacation.

The Apprentice was a phenomenally successful television show. It took a lot of people by surprise—myself included. It made a lot of people rich and famous, and it changed the way a lot of folks looked at their own careers. And if you believe some media pundits it even revived an entire television network. It lived at the crosshairs of business and pleasure, art and commerce, high-end and lowbrow. Almost overnight, it seemed, it became a part of the culture. Like it or not, I became a part of the culture right along with it, but I like to think I'm grounded enough to know that the dust will eventually settle and before long folks will forget I ever appeared on a reality television show. Before long, I'll be back to where I was when the show started, back in Chicago—new and improved, perhaps, and richer for the experience, but back to working my own opportunities and chasing my own dreams, on my own terms.

While I'm sort of on the subject, I can't shake wondering why we've taken to labeling programs like *The Apprentice* as reality television. Who coined that one? There's nothing reality-based about sending sixteen accomplished young professionals out onto the New York City streets to sell lemonade. There's nothing real about letting us manage a popular theme restaurant for one night and competing over the receipts, or sending us off on a scavenger hunt to locate and purchase a list of items at the best possible price, or challenging us to imagine an advertising campaign for a jet leasing company. And there's *definitely* nothing real about throwing us all together in a luxury apartment, asking us to live like college roommates and shutting us off from the rest of the world.

Reality? I don't think so. *The Apprentice* is a great show, don't get me wrong, and I'm thrilled to have been a part of its first season, but when you break it down, it's really more of a game show than reality. Better, it's a months-long job interview—probably the most elaborate in the annals of human resources. It's an entertaining test of wits and skill sets and strategies designed to highlight the contestants' strengths and weaknesses in a business setting. And as it happened, I came out on top, which if you accept the show's premise makes me the most qualified out of all sixteen applicants to make it to this final stage to run one of the companies in Donald Trump's vast empire. Me, I don't necessarily buy that. I truly believe that in important ways we all showed qualities that would have been an asset to Donald Trump's real-world business; it's just that in the end, I managed to outthink, outhustle, outmaneuver, and otherwise outperform the other candidates and come away on top.

Okay, so who am I? Well, I'm a businessman, first and foremost. I live and work in my hometown of Chicago. I grew up in a modest neighborhood in a southwest suburb of the city called Orland Park. I have three older sisters—Beth, Katie, and Karen—and there's not an entrepreneur in the bunch: one's a speech pathologist, one's a high school teacher, and one was off to medical school before switching gears to become a consultant. My parents, Edward and Gail, were both teachers who later on became public school administrators.

My father passed away several years ago, after he had seen me start my own business and achieve some measure of success as an entrepreneur but long before I threw in on *The Apprentice* and caught the ridiculous wave I'm riding now. Still, I know he would have been proud of me and the way I conducted myself on the show, and the way I'm hopefully shouldering the resultant attention, all of which is an extension of how I try to conduct myself when no one's watching. Of course, that pride cuts both ways. I'm enormously proud of my family and the choices they've made; they've all done great and noble things, but their backgrounds certainly do not suggest a gene pool that would produce a child so fiercely devoted to building businesses and making money. And yet that's what I do. That's what I've always done, even back in high school, and if it's up to me, that's what I'll do for the rest of my life. For a while there, I thought I'd be a lawyer, but I talked myself out of that as soon as I hit college, where I quickly realized that the life of a lawyer wouldn't be a whole lot of fun. I decided early on that as long as I was going to work for a living it would have to be a blast. I've since started and sustained two businesses, and rehabbed and developed several building projects in downtown Chicago. I've managed to pull a better-than-decent living out of these, while having the time of my life along the way. Over the years I've also developed my own style, my own way of dealing with other people, my own way of approaching each new situation and opportunity.

I never went to business school. I don't have that kind of mind. I've never even read a book on business or marketing or negotiating strategies, because I don't believe good business instincts can be taught. That's why they call them *instincts*. They can be rehearsed, refined, and refashioned to suit a different set of circumstances, but I've yet to come across a textbook situation that could be gotten through with any kind of textbook solution.

That said, I'm a big believer in sharing information, learning from your mistakes, and patterning your behavior on successful individuals who have already made their marks. There's a lot to consider in every business situation, and a lot to master, and there's enormous benefit to be taken from a role model or a mentor or even a peer. If you want to know the truth, that's the real reason I signed on for the *Apprentice* audition. The grand prize of a high-salaried job heading one of Donald Trump's companies sounded nice, but I was already making good money heading projects and businesses of my own. I didn't need a job so much as I wanted the experience. The kick of appearing on a prime time television show was just that, a kick. I didn't want to upend my life for the several months it would take to shoot the show just for the chance to be on television and all of a sudden get great tables at restaurants or free tickets to sold-out shows. No way. The real reason I wanted to be on the show—actually, the *only* reason—was to soak in what I could of Donald Trump, an innovative, risk-taking, media-savvy businessman who has become so wildly successful that even his name has come to symbolize success. There was a great side benefit, too, for a competitive guy like me, and that was the chance to compare my experience with that of a bunch of Harvard Business School types, to see if I could match wits and mettle with the sharpest young business minds the producers could find and work together as part of a team.

But to work alongside Donald Trump . . . that was the real attraction. It's like going from high school ball straight up to the major leagues. I didn't know the details of what we'd be doing, but I knew Mr. Trump would be directly involved, and I couldn't wait to pump him with questions, or to sit back and watch him consider a dilemma, or to engage him in whatever ways the show would allow. There was so much I wanted to learn, and I wanted to learn from the best. After all, you don't ask a poor guy how to get rich, right? You don't ask a fat guy how to stay thin. You go to the guy who's done it all and soak up what you can, and here I meant to be an absolute sponge.

> No one ever got bigger, faster, stronger, or better going up against the little guy.

Nowadays, people ask me all the time if I was afraid I'd get fired during all those trips to Mr. Trump's boardroom after my team had been beaten badly in one of the show's patented challenges. I tell them the truth. I was never afraid. There wasn't a time during the run of the show when I felt I *deserved* to be fired, but I knew it could happen, and if it did I would have been all right with it. Really. No one wants to get fired, but I knew each week that someone had to go, and one thing I learned from my father is never to be afraid of failure. All you can do is try your best, go for it, and if it happens for you, then that's great. If it doesn't, then that's okay too. Stand up tall. Do everything you can. Cover all the bases and hope for the best. That's how I tried to conduct myself during my time on the show. I tried to be the best I could be—not only the best businessperson but also the best person—and I believe that came across. All around me, there was backstabbing and infighting and finger-pointing, but I tried to take whatever high road was available. I saw no need to shoot someone down in order to pump myself up, so I played the game the way I ran my businesses back home—with humility, credibility, and adaptability. In the end, this strategy served me well, only it wasn't a strategy; it was who I am, as I hope you'll see if you read on.

All of which takes me in a roundabout way to the book you now hold in your hands. No, it's not a traditional business book. And no, it's not the story of my life, because I can't imagine there's anybody out there willing to sit still long enough to read the story of my life other than my sisters, my mother, and maybe a couple of college buddies who spent too much time drinking back in school to remember their own stories. Better to think of it as an inadvertent business book, shot through with firsthand experiences, written for people like me who tend to avoid such things but who nevertheless recognize the value in someone else's perspective. There is no one right way to start and grow a company or negotiate a lease or market a product or reinvent a business plan, but there are some ways that have worked out pretty well for me. Those same approaches worked well on *The Apprentice*, and they're not school-taught or store-bought or otherwise prepared or processed. They're just an extension of who I am, and—who knows?—maybe they'll work out pretty well for you too.

ONE

The Spirit of Enterprise

> The world is a business, Mr. Beale.
> It has been since man crawled out of the slime.
>
> −Paddy Chayefsky, *Network*

Ask any successful person to look back over the events of his or her life, and chances are there'll be a turning point of one kind or another. It doesn't matter if that success has come on a ball field or in a boardroom, in a research laboratory or on a campaign trail—it can usually be traced to some pivotal moment. A lightbulb over the head. A rude awakening. An unexpected turn.

Here's mine, and I set it here at the outset because it has informed every decision I've made since. I was a couple of months out of college, and a couple of months into my first career-oriented job. I'd waxed boats and rehabbed cars and worked all kinds of hustles as a student looking to pocket some cash (more on these efforts in just a few pages), but this was my first hitch in a real-world job, working for a big corporation in anything like a big way. I'd hired on with a commodity metals company as an outside salesman, which was actually an interesting career move considering I knew about as much about commodity metals as I knew about fertilizer or waste management or industrial bathroom supplies. That is, I knew crap. I even said as much when I went in for my interview, but the guy doing the hiring didn't seem to care. He liked that I was honest and young, and he liked how I came across.

From my perspective, there wasn't much to like about the job beyond the paycheck and the chance to try out a variety of sales strategies that would serve me well later, but I was coming to realize that a decent paycheck can make up for a whole lot. Ever since my graduation in May, I'd been holding out for a dream job at a dream salary, and it took me until August to realize that these dreams were pretty much a fantasy and I'd better grab what I could. One by one, all of my college buddies had taken these nothing-special entry-level jobs, pushing papers for $18,000 or $21,000 a year (and hating the work besides), and I'd turn up my nose and tell them I wasn't about to get out of bed for anything less than $50,000. That was my line, my attitude. I'd gotten used to earning good money in my summer jobs, working with my hands, calling my own shots, making my own hours and collecting full value on the back of my full effort, and I simply couldn't see the point in busting my butt for a salary only slightly better than minimum wage. I was full of myself and thought my time was worth more than that. (And in truth it was, even though I was probably too young and arrogant to realize it.)

Your credibility is your greatest asset.

Anyway, my friends joined the workforce and left me hanging, to where I started to think maybe they were onto something. Maybe I'd missed a meeting or a memo telling me to get on board before the world passed me by. As a practical matter, it wasn't as much fun hanging out by myself all day while my buddies went to work, and I kept thinking maybe they knew something I didn't. At some point in all this uncertainty, I finally realized that I should just shut up and get out of bed and get to work, telling myself that if I didn't like the first job I found, I could always find another.

It was around this time that the commodity metals gig turned up and I went for it. Like I said, I didn't know the first thing about metals. Hell, I didn't know the second thing, either, but I was a quick study. I told the guy with some confidence that I could sell anything, and I honestly believed that I could.

The job didn't quite pay $50,000, but if I succeeded, it would get me close. I had a company car at my disposal, an expense account, and a guaranteed salary of $30,000, plus commissions. Really, it was cush, and with any luck I figured I could push my take well over my $50,000 target. It was all I could do to keep from calling my buddies and telling them how smart I was for holding out.

One of the most interesting things about the job was that I was the youngest guy on the sales force. By about ten to fifteen years. All of the other salesmen were in their forties, and there I was, all of twenty-three, playing in the big leagues. These guys had kids and mortgages and car payments. Me, I was living with my parents, same house I'd grown up in, and all I was worried about was pizza and walking-around money, so the stakes were entirely different. To them, it was everything; to me, it was just an okay gig, a place to start.

There was a lot to learn. I'd sold myself as a salesman, but in truth I had no idea how to sell. I learned by watching, by listening to the sales pitches that worked and the ones that didn't, by modeling my demeanor on some of the more successful salesmen we had in the field. The good ones displayed a quiet confidence. They were never desperate to make a sale, which I eventually learned was because desperation never closed any deal. Their confidence came from knowing they had a good product at a good price, and because the deals they were offering were profitable all around. It's a lot easier to sell when you can stand behind your product or service and know you've got the goods.

I took to it well enough, learned what I needed to know about the metal business, scrambled to keep up with those veteran salesmen. There was an intensive thirty-day program to get me going, and I supplemented that with all kinds of reading and questions and extra effort. I may have been green going in, but I was solid and up to speed in no time at all. Even so, I didn't think I would ever have the confidence of some of these seasoned pros, but I wasn't about to admit this to anyone. The better move—indeed, the *only* move—was to strut my stuff, same as everyone else.

Turned out I could actually sell anything, once I learned the business and some surefire strategies, and it got to where I could work my route from ten in the morning to three in the afternoon and cover the same ground as everyone else. Since I was an outside salesman, seeing customers on my own, I took full advantage. These older guys were a trip—a regular bunch of Tin Men, for those of you who've ever seen the movie. For those of you who haven't . . . well, let's just say they were decent, hardworking, fun-loving guys, not above pulling a prank or two to keep things interesting or cutting a corner or two to keep them profitable. For a couple of months in there,

You are what you pretend to be.

all of us salesmen fell into a nice, easy routine where we'd meet at the health club by three each afternoon and chill. Actually, this had long been an established routine for the other salesmen; it just took me those first months to fall into it myself. I thought, Hey, this isn't bad for a first job. I could get used to this. I knew it would never make me rich and probably wouldn't make me happy, but it was a good first experience. I compared it to what my buddies were doing in their nothing-special jobs and felt pretty good about myself. They were working crazy hours and drawing nothing paychecks, to my nothing hours and crazy paychecks. I counted myself lucky, and whenever we got together at night I usually wound up buying, that's how guilty I felt for the easy time I was having.

Still, I wasn't challenged on the job, and it began to gnaw at me. I need to push myself in order to feel whole, and here the only push was to go through the same motions day after day. Sure, I could set and meet a quota, but I told myself there had to be more to my days than that. I was too young, energetic, and full of ideas to phone it in just yet. I'd learned my share of lessons to this point, and I would learn a bunch more—hey, I'm still learning!—but this turning point was the first tough lesson I had to consider. Shook me up to where I vowed never to be in the same position to get burned like the guy on the receiving end.

Here's what happened. There was a guy who'd been with the company for thirty years—senior management, one of the top brass. I knew him only by reputation. He'd worked his way to the top, and he still hadn't eased up on the gas. He was the first one there in the morning and the last one to leave in the evening, that's how focused and on top of things he was. Busted his ass for that company, and then woke up the next morning and busted it again. One day he reported early for work, business as usual, and he was met in his office by one of his superiors and a colleague. The two men had been sent to fire him, and they ended up escorting him from his office directly to the parking lot. This was a dedicated company guy, a thirty-year veteran, loyal as his career had been long, and they didn't even let him finish out the day.

That was tough enough, but the reason for his dismissal was even more confounding: his salary, which naturally had increased over the years, was too much for the company to handle. The head of the company figured he could hire two or three junior executives for what he was paying this pro, so he cut him loose. Just like that. I actually stood off to the side and watched as they walked this poor guy out to the parking lot, and it struck me as the most incongruous thing. I thought, Man, that sucks! And it truly did, big-time. To dedicate your life to a company, to bring in a ton of business and build lots of important relationships, only to be sent packing because the bottom line couldn't justify keeping you on.

Keep your options open. And remember, where there is no risk, there is no reward.

Of course I knew that firings such as this one happen all the time in corporate America—after all, the business pages of our daily newspapers are filled with stories of companies downsizing or casting off big-salaried veterans in favor of affordable rookies—but to see it play out with people you know is another story. Let me tell you, it was a real wake-up call, and I didn't want to stick around long enough to hear another. I'd been on the job only a short time, and I'd been thinking things were going well, but I watched this soap opera play itself out and realized there was no such thing as job security. Not selling metals, and not anywhere else. Thirty years of service don't mean a damn thing, and even though I wasn't planning on logging thirty years with this company, the notion of it still scared the crap out of me. I thought, What the hell am I doing, throwing in on a gig that could disappear on me at any time for any reason? What kind of fool would I be to stake my career on the good graces of a cold, heartless corporation? How could I continue to work in a place where being too successful would get me shown the door? Most of the world does work under just these terms, but then it occurred to me that as long as there wasn't any kind of security in the corporate world, I might as well operate without any kind of security on my own.

This realization was my epiphany. There is no such thing as job security when you work for someone else, so why not work for yourself? The lesson hit hard and pushed me to consider my next move. It seemed a no-brainer that I would stay on for a little longer while I cast about for another opportunity, but in every other respect I cut myself loose that very afternoon, and as I did so, I realized I was pretty much on my own. Hey, we're all pretty much on our own in whatever it is we do, and I figured I needed to accept this basic fact of business life and move on. No sense dwelling on events outside my control, I thought, and no sense leaving that control in the hands of someone else. Better to take control in what ways I could. From that moment forward I set about looking for opportunities that had my name on them, and my name alone. I'd continue to work in a corporate setting because I had to for the time being, but I wouldn't make my living there. I'd make it on my own.

I guess this is easier said than done, because if it really

was a no-brainer to make it on your own in business there'd
be millions of no-brained, harebrained, and otherwise dubi-
ously brained individuals quitting their day jobs and hanging
out their own shingles. Nobody would be left in the talent
pool to round out the workforce and execute the business
plan. So clearly, making it on your own is not easy. It's a
mind-set, really, and even as I embraced it for myself, I realized it's not for everyone. Some people are perfectly happy
working for others or are terrified of being out there on their
own, without the safety net of a steady paycheck. Many of
these folks are able to build interesting, challenging, even
entrepreneurial careers within a corporate setting, and I
have nothing but admiration and respect for those who manage to make the most out of whatever situation they find
themselves working in. It's just that in my case, I couldn't
see working for someone else any longer than I absolutely
had to; I couldn't see coming into work each morning and
wondering if I would still have a job at the end of the day; I
couldn't see busting my butt for a commission or a bonus
while the owner of the company earned the true windfall.

So what did I do? I wrapped my mind firmly around the
idea of setting out on my own. This sudden dismissal of a
man I hardly knew was the push that sent me on my own
path, and it's been a constant reminder that I can reach only
as high as the bar I set for myself. Could I have built a nice
career at that metals company, logging my own thirty years
and earning my own hefty commissions and building my own
lifetime of contacts? Probably. Could I have made a decent
living? Again, probably, but I never would have been anything more than a company guy, a salesman, and there would
always have been a ceiling on what I could hope to earn. And
more to the point, this success could always have been taken

away from me at any time—for good reason or for no reason at all—and this last fact was a deal-breaker as far as I was concerned.

The comedian Chris Rock does a great riff on the difference between being successful and being wealthy, and it's relevant here. Shaquille O'Neal, he says, is successful. He makes tens of millions playing basketball—as of this writing, for the Los Angeles Lakers. He can buy anything and everything he wants. Even if he never plays another game, he'll never have to worry about money. But Jerry Buss, the owner of the Los Angeles Lakers? The man who signs Shaq's paycheck? He's wealthy. The distinction is huge. Shaquille O'Neal can become the highest paid athlete in the history of professional sports, but he's still a hired gun. The guy who signs his checks will always do the math and weigh what he can afford to pay his star player against what he can hope to make as a result of employing that athlete. Shaq can be the

Never give up.

most physically powerful player in the game, Chris Rock maintains, but Jerry Buss will always have the power, and I decided at this crossroads that I would seek that same position of power.

Now, I realize that everything is relative. I know that Shaq can buy and sell me a thousand times over, and that there are a great many corporate executive types who have achieved a level of success that might be forever out of my reach. But for me, that's not the point. For me, the key comes in the reaching. (More on this later.) After seeing the way this commodity metals company treated one of its own, I wasn't about to work for anyone but myself, in tireless support of anyone's bottom line but my own. No, there is no such thing as job security. Never has been. Never will be. That's the hard, plain truth of it, and if we mean to make it in the world of business, we need to get beyond this simple fact of business life. It doesn't mean you shouldn't work for someone else, just that you shouldn't assume your job will always be there waiting for you. And it doesn't mean that going it alone is right for everybody. It isn't. But get the point, and move on from there, and you'll never get a wake-up call like this salesman on his last day of work.

There's another harsh lesson I want to mention here. This one found me almost ten years later, in Donald Trump's boardroom on the set of *The Apprentice*. Once again, there were sixteen candidates vying for the same job, which meant that fifteen of us would be sent packing one by one. We'd work in teams, on a variety of assignments set up as competitions, and at the end of each task the members of the winning team were advanced to the next round, while the members of the losing team had to defend their actions and decisions, knowing that one of their group would be fired in order to winnow the field.

The difficult realization here came in the shifting alliances and allegiances that surfaced among us. Teammates would sell each other out in order to save their own hides. Or conversely, they'd sing each other's praises in hopes of winning praise in return. Mr. Trump would ask us to assess each other's performances and our own, and the responses were telling. Predictable, perhaps, but also telling. No one would take credit for a misstep or second-guess his or her own initiative, while everyone was quick to point fingers and lay blame. It was a full-in-the-face reminder of another simple fact of business life: No one can be trusted. And yet trust is an essential component of any successful business team, which left me to wonder: If you can't rely on your colleagues to cover your back and set you straight, how can you ever hope to accomplish your shared goals?

Indeed, the cover-your-butt mentality of the workplace will get you only so far. The follow-your-gut mentality of the entrepreneur has the potential to take you anywhere you want to go or run you right out of business—but it's a whole lot more fun, don't you think?

Lessons Learned
ON GOALS

START WHERE YOU WANT TO FINISH Visualize yourself at the top of whatever mountain you're hoping to scale and you're already on your way. I can't tell you how many frustrated young professionals I've encountered who work their butts off and still never seem to get anywhere in their careers. Why? Well, you never *really* know why some folks go the distance and some only tread water, but I have an idea it comes down to focus and clarity. After all, if there's no clear goal in mind, how can you ever expect to reach it? If you mean to be financially independent by the age of thirty-five, then say so. Set about it. Write it down. Tape it to your bathroom mirror or to the visor on your car. The constant reminder will keep you focused and on track, and will encourage you to work backwards from your target to discover the steps you'll need to take in order to get the job done.

BREAK THE JOURNEY INTO SMALLER, ACHIEVABLE MILESTONES Sometimes a far-off goal can appear so out of reach you can't be bothered. On a football field, for example, the quarterback doesn't think goal line every time he calls a play. It's all about eating up yardage—three yards here, seven yards there—and buying your team time to keep possession and continue marching down the field. Every ten yards, you get another few chances to move toward that goal line. Running a business or charting a career is a lot like an eighty-yard scoring drive. Even better, it's similar to running a marathon. You can't expect to reach the finish line without passing twenty-six mile markers along the way; there's no avoiding them, so you might as well set your sights on them. I've completed two Chicago Marathons, and I'm hoping to run a bunch more, and each time out I've brought the long haul down to size by breaking the distance into these doable increments. We get where we're going one step at a time, one mile at a time, one initiative at a time.

KEEP YOUR BALANCE We need to mix things up in order to keep things interesting, both at home and in the office, so I try to recognize the lifestyle choices that run alongside every career move I consider. Will this opportunity keep me from my friends and family? Will I be on the road constantly, to where I'll never have time to pursue outside interests? Will I burn the candle at both ends in such a way that I burn myself out as well? Whatever you set out to do, make sure that the doing is something you can handle—indeed, something you *want* to handle. There should be joy in the work, and room enough outside of work for joy in the rest of your life as well.

BET THE LONG SHOT Life and business are all about succeeding against the odds, and sometimes it seems those odds are stacked impossibly against you. When you apply for your first job, you'll compete with dozens of candidates, maybe hundreds. And what are the odds of finding the perfect life partner or raising a happy, healthy family? Truth is, if we let ourselves be intimidated by slim chances we'd never take risks. Human nature suggests we play it safe. Only the last time I checked, the sure thing never paid off any better than even money, so I'm always thinking home run or Hail Mary pass as the clock winds down. Inch forward when you can, but always keep an ace up your sleeve.

KNOW THE ANSWER BEFORE YOU ASK THE QUESTION The successful entrepreneur is never surprised, not even by the most unexpected turn. At each step, on each task, think things through to where every eventuality is apparent. This doesn't mean you don't take risks or try something new, but you do so from a place of knowing. Or at least from a place of *best guessing*. Anticipate every outcome, consider every possibility, and you're in a better position to handle whatever comes next.

CELEBRATE YOUR ACHIEVEMENTS When all goes well, clap yourself on the back. You deserve it. If you find yourself in a leadership role, make sure to reward your team at every turn. They deserve it. If you're a team player, remind your colleagues of your success, and talk it up like it matters, because it most certainly does. And if you're flying solo, find a point of pause and give yourself a big thumbs-up. We've all heard that old saying "Nothing succeeds like success." But what we sometimes fail to realize is that success in a vacuum is just another day at the office.

TWO

Getting Started

If you don't drive your business,
you will be driven out of business.

—B. C. Forbes

S ome of my earliest childhood memories have to do
with money. Earning it, counting it, saving it, and soon
enough, investing it. More to the point, these memories have to do with how much I seemed to *enjoy* making
money, as if it were a game of some kind, a challenge, and I
suppose that's how it has been, from a very early age. Anyway, that's the punch line to more family stories than I care
to remember, which leaves me running with it here, in these
early pages.

Now, I don't want folks thinking I was all about money
all the time—like an Orland Park version of Michael J. Fox's
character in *Family Ties*. It wasn't like that at all, but I was
wired a little differently from my parents and my sisters and
most of the other neighborhood kids, and for some reason
the stories that get passed around at our family gatherings
portray me with dollar signs in my eyes.

Here's one: I was nine or ten years old and visiting my
grandmother and I wasn't too happy about it. My parents
were out of town for the weekend, and they thought I was too

young to stay alone with my sisters, so they shipped me off to Grandma Rancic's. After about ten minutes, I was bored out of my mind. My grandmother lived by herself, and she was happy for the company, but there was nothing for me to do, so on Saturday morning she hit on the idea of teaching me how to cook. This, it turned out, was a genius move. Grandma Rancic loved to cook. She taught me how to make her special pancakes, and the time just flew. Let me tell you, at the end of the day, I was all over those pancakes. I was the pancake master.

Next morning, I was feeling so good about my pancakes I encouraged my grandmother to invite some of her friends over for breakfast. I guess I wanted to show off a little, maybe get some pinches on the cheek. It was an innocent, genuine offer—a chance to strut and nothing more. So she called five or six of her friends—most of them widows like herself, most of them from Croatia, which was where my paternal grandparents were from. Sure enough, these women were also eager for the company, and they hurried over to Grandma Rancic's house. They all had names like Mania and Frances, and they all spoke with thick Croatian accents. There was an awful lot of kissing as I recall, but the pancakes were a big hit. My grandmother's friends seemed to enjoy themselves, and my grandmother was certainly in her element and loving it. I was having a good time too.

When it came time for all the ladies to leave, I said goodbye and returned to the kitchen to clear the table and do the dishes. When I did, I noticed that each and every one of my grandmother's friends had slipped a five-dollar bill underneath her plate. It was the most remarkable thing. So what did I do? Pretty much what any self-respecting ten-year-old would have done: I pocketed the money and kept quiet.

The very next weekend, I asked my parents if I could go visit Grandma Rancic again. My father was probably delighted that I had found some point of connection with her, and only too happy to take me for another visit, and as soon as I got there I told my grandmother to invite her friends for Sunday breakfast. What had been innocent and genuine only the week before was now something else entirely. The pancake master was back, and I was hoping these women were still hungry. (And still flush!) They once again trooped over to my grandmother's, and each slipped a second five-dollar bill beneath her plate before she left, and I figured I was onto something. Realize, this was back in 1980 or so, and five dollars was pretty steep for a stack of pancakes, but it never occurred to me that I was fleecing these sweet old ladies out of their Social Security checks. If I thought about it at all, I suppose I just assumed that all elderly Croatian ladies were in the habit of showering money on their friends' grandchildren. Maybe it was some kind of custom.

> **W**ork every opportunity to full advantage.

Now, looking back, I'm sure my grandmother was hip to what was happening, but we never talked about it. She never asked for a piece of the action, and I didn't think to cut her in, even though it would have been good business to kick back something for the cost of the ingredients and the room rental and the marketing to my "patrons." (If I had been more of a schemer, I probably would have thought to pay her some hush money, just to keep her from telling my parents what I was up to.) For Grandma Rancic's part, she was probably just thrilled that I was spending all of this time with her and left it at that.

Things went on in this way a couple of times more until eventually my mother stumbled across my hard-earned stash one day while she was cleaning my room. I must have collected over a hundred dollars by this point, which was a lot of money for a kid, and when she asked me about it, I came clean. I told her I was running a makeshift restaurant out of Grandma Rancic's kitchen, and Grandma and I were both in for a good talking-to. I was forced to look for a new line of work.

This was my first taste of capitalism, my first significant payday, my first incentive to hustle for more of the same. Turned out I liked making money, and I liked the motivation to succeed, and I especially liked the fact that people would pay you for something you'd just as soon do for free. The only problem was that once I'd gotten paid for it, I wasn't all that interested in cooking breakfast for all those ladies unless there was something in it for me. I was too young to understand any larger picture. My thinking was, Why give away the store? I don't mean to sound mercenary, but back then the money was the most compelling part of the deal. If you eliminated it from these pancake breakfasts, the entire enterprise was a whole lot less interesting.

> **W**hen you stumble across a gold mine, be sure to retrace your steps so you can stumble across it again.

Predictably, that story was trotted out over the years, whenever my parents felt they needed to explain how two educators could have given birth to a budding tycoon. My mother got a mess of mileage out of it once *The Apprentice* hit the airwaves, although to tell the truth, I never saw anything remarkable in the tale. To me, it was the most natural thing in the world, once these sweet little old ladies started digging deep, to repeat whatever it was that had persuaded them to give me their money in the first place. No, I didn't set out to make a buck, but I got used to it pretty quick.

Here's another story, one that has nothing to do with money and everything to do with the imaginative ways in which I tend to look at the world; if you're meaning to make some noise as an innovative entrepreneur, I suspect the two go hand in hand. In the spring of my kindergarten year, my teacher sent home a note asking my mother to make an appointment to discuss my progress. When my mother showed up for the appointment, she was met by my kindergarten teacher, the school psychologist, a special education teacher, and the school principal. My poor mother remembers feeling ambushed. Of course, she knew who the principal was, but she didn't have the slightest notion what these other professionals were doing sitting in on what she'd been led to believe was a garden-variety parent-teacher conference. As these people took turns introducing themselves, she began to fidget. She wondered, What has Billy been up to now?

Apparently, what I'd been up to was coloring outside the lines. Literally. My mother saved some of my drawings, and some of it was sloppiness, but here and there you could see that, even at five years old, I would not be bound by expectation. If I thought a predetermined shape should be taller or fatter or otherwise bigger, I made it so. I don't think I was being difficult or obstinate—in fact, I'm sure I wasn't—but I guess I saw things a certain way, and when they didn't jibe with the accepted approach I went with my best judgment. Or I just kept scribbling, without rules or boundaries.

Nowadays, to color outside the lines has become a metaphor for thinking outside the box, for refusing to be hemmed in by convention, but back then, it meant I couldn't follow simple instructions. It was a negative instead of a positive, and these well-meaning people were concerned. The special ed teacher suggested I be tested for a learning disability, because I couldn't even confine my handwriting to the lines on our ruled notepaper, but it was agreed that the first step would be for me to have my eyes checked. My mother, who as I mentioned was also a teacher, was inclined to go through the motions even though she hadn't seen any indications of a problem in my writing or coloring or eyesight up to this point, so she took me to see her ophthalmologist. As it happened, this guy couldn't find anything wrong with my eyesight, and at some point in the examination he turned to my mother and said, "Why did you bring him here?"

"His teachers said he doesn't color inside the lines," my mother explained. "His handwriting is all over the place too."

The doctor assured my mother my eyes were fine and suggested that perhaps my teachers needed to assess their students and their capabilities in creative new ways.

And that's how it was. Everyone else in my family toed the line and followed instructions. Me, I crossed the line and looked for opportunities—to try something new, to test the limits, to swim against the current. I even had a sixth grade teacher who called my mother in to tell her I should think about pursuing a career in one of the trades because I was never going to amount to anything academically. Now, as an adult, I look back on that kind of tossed-off assessment and cringe, because I was pretty much like every other kid in this lady's class. Our interests lay mostly outside the classroom, and we all counted the minutes until the final bell each afternoon. Nevertheless, my mother was concerned. Education was a big deal in our household. School came first and foremost, and it was always assumed that all four of us kids would go directly to college after high school. To hear from this sixth grade teacher that I should probably consider a different course was alarming to my parents, who had always thought of me as bright and inquisitive. It was alarming, that is, until my mother secured a second opinion from my social studies teacher. She maintained that I was an insightful, original, and critical thinker, with writing skills that had simply not yet caught up with my oral communication skills.

> **K**now your limits. Recognize your opportunities. And put the two together to make a good fit.

By the time I was in high school, there were other matters to occupy my attention. I was reading the *Robb Report* and *Barron's* when everyone else was reading *Sports Illustrated* and *Playboy*. I no longer recall how I came across these publications in the first place—probably some well-meaning relative wanting to reinforce an interest I expressed—but once I did, I was all over them. Don't misunderstand, I studied the box scores and rooted for the White Sox, same as the other South side kids, but I also studied the stock tables and followed the action on the Chicago Mercantile Exchange. My teachers had stopped suggesting remedial course work, and my handwriting had managed to improve on its own, but making money was still very much on my mind, and the older I got, the more money seemed to matter.

As I moved on in school, I became all too aware of some of the class differences between me and some of the other kids—differences that didn't seem to matter back in kindergarten but that became an issue as I reached into adolescence and beyond. At some point, roughly coinciding with adolescence, we kids started to divide ourselves along class lines. There were the haves and the have-nots and the somewhere-in-betweens. We Rancics weren't poor, not by any stretch. We lived in a nice house. We wore nice clothes and attended good private schools. We even took some great family vacations. Ours was an extremely loving, comfortable household, and we Rancic kids didn't want for much. But by the standards of some of the kids I was going to school with, we checked in at the modest level, at about the time I came to appreciate what it meant to drive a nice car or wear a styling new pair of sneakers or listen to music on a kick-ass stereo.

> **D**on't waste your time coveting your neighbors' assets. It's better to invest your time in the fruitful pursuit of your own goals.

None of those things really mattered in any kind of grand scheme, but when you're a gangly teenager anxious to fit in at a school where most kids came from some of Chicago's nicest neighborhoods, these things *seem* to matter more than anything else.

I meant to do something about it. My parents didn't have the money to buy me my own car, which like it or not was the defining status symbol among my group of friends. In our crowd, you were what you drove, and that's just how it was. And yet even if my parents had that kind of money, I'm not so sure they would have looked on a car as a reasonable expense; there were other ways to get around, and other priorities. Anyway, I was on my own in terms of transportation. To put a fine point on it, I was on my own for all of my "nonessential" expenses, but a car was the first big-ticket item that threatened to break my piggy bank, and I was desperate to find a sweet set of wheels that would at least come close to what some of my buddies were driving. About the best I could manage was a beat-up silver Audi Fox, a four-door sedan that had its back window blown out and enough dings in the doors to scare off most other buyers. The seller was asking $600 for it, which was about what he needed to get out from under and about what I could afford, so we shook on it. I was fifteen years old. I'd saved some money from various odd jobs over the years and hoarded the cash I'd sometimes get for birthday and Christmas presents. Pretty much all of it was earmarked for my first car. I didn't even have my license yet, but I was planning ahead. My thinking was I could probably find a rear window at a junkyard and figure a way to install it myself, at which point I'd be well ahead of the game and somewhat better than roadworthy by the time my sixteenth birthday rolled around. At the time, my father was driving a Chevy Caprice and my mother a Chevy Impala station wagon, so once I cleaned up my silver Audi Fox and replaced the window, it would be the most happening car in our driveway.

I dragged my second cousin, Mark Skau, to a couple of city junkyards to help me locate the right window. We called around first to see who might have the part, and then we followed up in person. Mark was in town on a visit and happy to be put to work. Also, he was older, so I assumed he knew what he was doing, although in truth neither one of us had the first idea how to install a rear window in a car. We didn't even know who to ask! I finally located the window, which cost me about $50, and hauled it back to my parents' house, where Mark and I went to work on it. We lathered that thing with enough Ivory to clean a football team, trying to lubricate it sufficiently so we could snap it in beneath the fittings, but it was a real struggle. There was no instruction booklet, nobody to walk us through it, just two idiots on a nice street in Orland Park, Illinois, trying to squeeze a square peg into a round hole. Really, first hour or so into the job, it didn't seem we would *ever* get that window into place, but we soaped that thing up in such a way that a couple of hours later we finally got it in.

We weren't too sure about the installation when we were through. My cousin remarked that I should probably make sure the windows were down whenever I closed the doors, so the rear window wouldn't pop out from the trapped pressure, and he was probably right to worry. I never found out for certain because I wound up selling the car just a week or so after we'd finished with it. I meant to drive it myself as soon as I had a license, but we'd washed it and waxed it and cleaned it up to where I started to get offers I felt I had to consider. I mean, I'd gotten it at such a distress-sale price that I was looking at a nice profit, so I struck a deal with a gas station owner I knew who had a prominent corner location in town, at LaGrange Road and 143rd Street, and he let me leave the car out in front with a FOR SALE sign in the window to attract customers.

Reaching out to this gas station owner was a valuable lesson in itself, one that has been reinforced throughout my career. I knew the guy only because that station was where my parents tended to buy gas, but I had no real relationship with him. Still, he seemed approachable enough, and his station was situated on a prime corner in town, so I just wandered by one afternoon and put it to him straight. I didn't offer to cut him in on my deal, and he didn't ask. I suppose if he had, I would have considered it, but I presented it as more of a favor than a business deal. I said something like "Hey, I'm trying to sell this thing. Okay if I park it here for a couple days, see what turns up?"

Within a week, I ended up selling the car for $1,200 to a college student who had stopped by to check it out. A $550 profit, not counting our sweat equity, in just a week or so, all because I'd thought to create value from no value at all. All because I had come across an owner who needed to sell at a time

> **L**earn the rules of the game, and reinvent them if they don't apply.

when I'd had the money and the foresight to buy, and because I had thought to "market" my wares at a high-profile location. And all because I was willing to part with something that had all of a sudden become more valuable to someone else than it was to me.

The beauty of this first transaction was that I actually managed to sell the same car twice, making this yet another story my parents got a kick out of repeating. This first buyer took the car home to show it to his father, who proceeded to flip a gasket. He didn't think his son could afford the car or the insurance or the upkeep, and he called to see if I would take it back. Even at fifteen, I knew how to negotiate from strength. This father wanted to get his son out from under and quick, so I didn't offer to refund *all* of his money. I wasn't out to stick it to these good people, but I didn't want to stick it to myself either. After all, it would have been crazy to give all that money back, under just these circumstances, so I told this man that I had costs involved in restoring the car. This was true enough. I told him I had turned down other offers once I had accepted his son's offer, and that I had lost some significant selling opportunities in the several days since I'd taken the car off the market—also, true enough. I told him I had partners to consider—not quite true, but here I was thinking I could mention my cousin or this gas station owner, even though neither one of them was expecting a penny from the sale. I didn't have it in me to lie, but I could stretch the truth with the best of them, and after some back-and-forth the father agreed to let me keep $400 if I took back the car. So that's what I did. Here again, I don't mean to come off as a moneygrubbing kid, but in wanting to be fair to this man and his son I didn't want to lose sight of the fact that I needed to be fair to myself.

Stick to your principles, but always keep an open mind.

Like I said, my father got a big charge out of that story—and so did I once I parked that silver Audi Fox back at the gas station and put the FOR SALE sign back in the window. I asked for the same $1,200 I received on the first deal, and this time I put my asking price right on the sign, thinking this would save me time and hassle if anyone called to inquire. I don't think I fully understood about negotiating strategies when I was fifteen, but I was beginning to get a feel for recognizing a bargain and developing an upper hand, and I knew enough to ensure that when a potential buyer called he would at least be interested in the car at something close to my asking price. It would mean I had a "warm" buyer; it would then fall to me to turn up that heat and make the sale. And that's just how it happened. Someone called to ask about the car. I knew he had seen the price, so when he didn't mention the price I was able to assume we were close on terms. After all, *he* was calling *me*, so he must have found something to like in the deal, and I was able to convert the very first call into a sale—at full price.

In a matter of two weeks, then, I had laid out $600 for a beat-up car with a blown-out window, sank another $50 and some elbow grease into a new window, washed and waxed the car to where you didn't notice the dings in the door, and positioned it on a prominent corner in town. And I somehow managed to sell the damn thing twice! Once for $400, and the next time for $1,200—in all, a profit of close to $1,000.

I thought, Man, that was easy! And it was. There was some genuine hard work and a little risk, but it was a relatively easy transaction with a substantial payoff. I looked around at all my buddies delivering pizzas or flipping burgers or working some other minimum wage job and it seemed to me they were out of their minds, to work so long and so hard for so little. I'd stuck my neck out, but in creating value, in buying low and selling high and turning opportunity to advantage, I'd made my own little killing, and the lesson was not lost on me. In fact, it was such a sweet deal I immediately went out in search of another car, on the sound thinking that if the formula worked once, it would work again. I picked up a copy of *The Trading Times*, which was filled with classified ads from folks wanting to buy and sell just about anything in the Chicago area. Cars, ski equipment, room air conditioners . . . it was like a swap meet in print, and I felt sure I could find another lowball deal to match my first. I also bought a copy of the Blue Book that car dealers use to gauge shifts in the resale market; it has a book valuation for virtually every make and model of car. With these tools I was ready to tackle the marketplace.

An activity that had started out of necessity, as the only

way I could afford a car, had quickly turned into a hobby, and soon enough it would turn into a kind of business. I didn't recognize it as such at the time, but that's what it was, make no mistake. I was all over Chicago, checking out cars, answering ads, talking to all kinds of strange people, and it never occurred to me until recently what an odd picture I must have made, at fifteen, peeling off twenties and fifties from my bankroll as if I were a big-time wheeler-dealer. I wasn't even old enough to drive, so I had to get rides to keep these appointments around town, which strikes me now as odd, but I guess it just confirms that you're never too old to think for yourself or to strike out on your own.

I wasn't out looking to take advantage of anybody—heck, I was fifteen! how could I take advantage of anybody?—but I was looking to take advantage of certain situations. There's a difference. If someone needed quick cash and was offering to sell his car below book value, I didn't think it was up to me to talk him out of it. It wasn't up to me to offer full price. I'd check out the car, determine what it was worth to me, what I might be able to get for it after I had fixed it up, and make my best offer. If the seller grabbed at it, it was on him and not on me; we would have arrived at the precise tipping point of the transaction, the most I could afford up against the least he could take, and we would have a deal.

> In a negotiation, you must always be prepared to walk away from a deal.

About a week or so later, I found another deal that would allow me to take the basic principle of supply and demand out for another test drive. I set my sights on a 1979 Datsun 280Z, a sporty two-seater that could have put me in the same league as some of my buddies, who were driving new Mustang GT convertibles and Monte Carlo SS coupes. The 280Z would likely be the best car I could afford, so I put some money into it beyond the purchase price. I found someone selling a secondhand car stereo and equalizer and made him an offer, thinking once again I could install the thing myself. And once again, I didn't have the first clue how to go about it, so I roped in one of my best friends, Darren Haramija, to help me figure it out. Darren had a really cool Jeep with a killer stereo—man, I *loved* that car!—and as we worked on my Z, I imagined some other kid from the neighborhood looking on at my tricked-out ride and wishing he had one just like it, the same way I'd been wishing on Darren's Jeep.

This time, I ended up keeping the car for a few months. As a matter of fact, that Z was my ride when I first got my license, and it was a great source of pride, but I'd done such a good job fixing it up I kept getting offers on it. Finally I had to sell. Rode it over to that same gas station on the corner, slapped another sign in the window, and within a couple days I'd doubled my money yet again.

That's how it was with me and cars, pretty much through high school. Turning three-figure purchases into four-figure sales, driving one car until another turned up at an attractive price, and putting the surplus into my next fixer-upper. In this way I managed to sock away some serious cash by the end of my senior year and to buy bigger and better cars each time out. I never again made as much on the flip as I did that first time around, with that silver Fox I managed to sell twice, but there was good money to be made—at least a couple of hundred dollars on each transaction. I ran through seven or eight cars by the time I graduated, and my parents were caught somewhere between admiring my pluck and resourcefulness to worrying that I'd be seduced by the apparently easy money I was making. Really, it shouldn't have been so easy, but it was, and at one point I added up all the money I'd made on these used-car transactions and realized I would have had to work at McDonald's for two years, full-time and at minimum wage, to even get close to what I was making. That was precisely my parents' worry. They thought I was having such a smooth go of it I'd see no reason to go to college. They thought I'd wind up a used-car salesman—not a bad thing to be, but not exactly what they had in mind, at least not just yet.

At fifteen, then, I learned the art of buying low and selling high. I stumbled across it, really, and I couldn't have attached a name to what I was doing at the time, but I'd put a basic principle to work because it was just that, basic. It made sense. You learn a whole lot about people when they're selling their cars, and there were different ways I had to present myself to each. I wasn't sophisticated enough to think to dress the part, and even if I was, my wardrobe consisted mainly of jeans and T-shirts, but I became a student of human nature. It got to where I could spot someone who *needed* to sell just from the desperation I could read into their ad; without fully realizing what I was doing, I traded on that desperation in order to strike a deal.

Start small, think big, and aim somewhere in between.

Early on, I figured out that the best move was to make a lowball offer, but to make it without insulting the owner. I'd say something like, "Look, man, I'd love to get into that car, but this is all I can swing right now." Most times, the guy would blow me off if I came in too much below his asking price, but I learned that this was okay. This was part of the dance. I'd give him my name and number and tell him if he wasn't able to get his price to give me a call. I'd be respectful and professional, and more times than I can count I got a call back a couple weeks later, asking if I was still interested—at *my* price.

You can't fall in love with a car and expect to land it on your terms. I'm sorry, but you just can't. This is true in all business transactions. Fall in love with that oceanfront property at your own peril, because it won't let you think clearly about the merits of the deal. When you get emotionally attached to whatever it is you're negotiating, you're screwed. I was always prepared to walk away. I offer this as a strategy, but with a lot of these cars it wasn't a strategy so much as it was a constraint. I always looked at cars just out of my reach, so I knew going in that the only way I could swing a deal was if the guy came down substantially in his price. If he couldn't or wouldn't, I'd move on to the next listing in the classifieds. And there was *always* a next listing in the classifieds, so it made no sense getting all worked up over any one deal.

Also, I tried to approach each deal as a win-win situation, whether I was buying or selling. As a buyer, I looked past the dirt, grime, and broken windows to find a gem of a car underneath, something I could clean up and trick out in such a way that I was truly creating value, at a price where it was worth my while. As a seller, I looked to maximize the return on my investment, by marketing the car at the gas station or installing a secondhand stereo or springing for new tires or anything else I thought might make the car more attractive to the greatest number of potential buyers. Again, there was nothing new in my approach, except that I came by it on my own. No books, no courses, no mentor to guide me. Just drive, determination, and common sense—and a teenager's view that anything was possible.

As it turned out, the benevolent gas station owner built himself a nice little side business on the back of my idea. Folks noticed my cars parked in his lot and before long started asking him for the same arrangement, and after his handshake deal with me he started charging for the privilege—either a straight parking fee or a percentage of the deal. He never charged me, though, and I always considered it a justification of my instincts, the way the other car dealers caught on to my obvious approach and the way the gas station owner discovered all of this newfound money. Really, these deals were win-win-win situations.

Help your partners discover their dreams, and they'll help you to realize yours.

My parents continued to worry. They worried about the easy-money mentality I seemed to now carry. They worried about the seedy element they thought I was dealing with. They worried about the stereotypical image of the used-car salesman. And beneath each worry was a profound concern. This wasn't the life they imagined for me. This wasn't how things were meant to be. I was meant to focus on school, to get into a good college. The talk around the family dinner table—some of it fueled by me, I'll allow—was that I'd go to law school. There were lawyers in the family, and when I saw my way to a career, that's what I saw myself doing. I wanted to be in a courtroom, making a difference, never realizing that most lawyers wind up pushing papers and reviewing contracts. But as high school graduation approached, I was spending more and more of my time on these car deals—making good money, to be sure, but putting off a real game plan for college and beyond.

Oh, I would go to college. There was no question about that. But I would continue to color outside the lines, to steer clear of what was expected in favor of something new, to question conventional wisdom until I could back it up with personal experience. I wasn't sure I really wanted to be a lawyer, but I had no definite goal. All I knew was that each deal would get me one step closer to it, whatever it turned out to be.

Lessons Learned
ON VALUES

DON'T SELL YOURSELF AS SOMEONE YOU'RE NOT
Be careful how you present yourself, because it might come back to bite you. When I threw in on this metals sales job, I made it clear to my bosses that I had never done this type of work before, and I think they appreciated my honesty. A lot of the guys I wound up working with had conned their way into their positions, but I couldn't see coming to work each day on the back of a lie and hoping to not be found out. Better to come clean right out of the gate and let those doing the hiring decide if they want you as is, instead of as you present yourself. Remember, as I learned here, your bosses will never need a good reason to fire you, but you'd do well not to give them any ammunition just the same.

ACCEPT GOOD FORTUNE WITH GOOD CHEER An unlikely yield can leave you thinking of ways to achieve more of the same, but sometimes it's best to leave well enough alone. If I'd gone out and aggressively mined the deep pockets of my grandmothers' friends, I would have gone from cute to monstrous in the time it takes to pinch a cheek. If, as happened, I simply repeated the motions that resulted in the initial boon and hoped for the best, I could have counted myself lucky for the experience alone. Do what you love, for reasons other than the end, and you will always come out ahead.

KNOW THYSELF Yeah, I know, this is basic stuff, but you'd be amazed how many young people set off on their career paths without fully realizing who they are or where they come from or what they're hoping to get out of and put into their working lives. The answer for most of us lies back home, at the feet of our parents, in the communities that shaped us, with the neighbors who helped to raise us. After all, if you don't have a foundation, what are you going to stand on? The key to knowing what we're looking for comes in knowing where we come from, so make a thorough accounting.

NURTURE LIFELONG FRIENDSHIPS Successful entrepreneurs like to tally up their accounts on a regular basis, but the truly successful count their friends among their greatest assets. My father, a lifelong academic, always stressed the importance of fellowship. He helped us kids to recognize the value of a true and trusted friend, and to hold our friends close. As I move forward in my career I look back at the tremendous friendships I've built and sustained along the way. Hey, I'm still in close touch with some guys I have known since first grade! As lasting legacies go, these relationships are more important than any business or property I'll ever build. Unlike some of the dot-com companies that came and went at the turn of the last century, a great friendship can't be overvalued, and I'm expecting these investments to pay off for a lifetime.

ASK FOR HELP Most people are too embarrassed to reach out to others in a position to offer an assist, but folks will often surprise you. Or you might be disappointed, but that shouldn't keep you from asking in the first place. In the case of my first car, I was able to put a win-win proposition to the gas station owner, but there have been other times throughout my career when I've been on the receiving end of a generous turn where there was nothing in it for the other guy except the good karma that may or may not have come his way as a result. I've tried to keep this in mind on both ends of the equation. I'll seek advice, experience, insight, and even financial support from those who seem to have same in plenty—and I'll give it in return, if at all possible. What's in it for me? Everything.

KEEP A LITTLE SOMETHING FOR YOURSELF If you bend to every demand, there'll be nothing left to justify the transaction. And yet if you demand everything, there'll be no transaction. There's a great episode of *Taxi* in which Louie De Palma, the character played by Danny DeVito, is given an opportunity to literally fill in a blank check to complete a deal, and he pulls out his few remaining hairs in coming up with a figure. He knows there's a number that will make his benefactor balk, and another that will make him sigh with relief that the figure didn't come in any higher, and the dilemma comes in determining the very highest dollar amount Louie can justify without killing the deal. It's played to comic effect on the show, but there's a resonant truth to it. I'm not suggesting you gouge your customers or underpay your employees, but take the time to find the precise middle where both sides profit. When you're in business for the long haul, repeat business will be your keystone. See that it's still there when you come calling that second time.

BE A GOOD SPORT I was never much for that win-at-all-costs mind-set. Competitive sports were a big deal in my household growing up, and I was as competitive as anyone I knew, but to me there was no joy in beating an opponent into the ground. When an upstart outfit surfaced to give my cigar business a run for its money, for example, we redoubled our efforts in order to maintain our market share, but there was no need to quash the other guys in order to lift our fortunes. There was no venom or rancor in the chase. It was good, healthy competition, and it made us stronger, leaner, and more attuned to the marketplace.

SAY WHAT YOU MEAN AND MEAN WHAT YOU SAY Keep your word. Honor your commitments and they will double back to honor you. Let's face it, without credibility and personal integrity, it doesn't matter what you've built or bought or sold. You're only as strong as your promises kept. If you're riding high, and you mean to stay there, make certain to deliver on your promises, to back up every claim, and to make yourself abundantly clear.

BUILD RELATIONSHIPS We stand on so many sets of shoulders in order to succeed, it's a wonder we don't topple over, and yet too often we do our climbing without any real regard for the folks lending the assist. Keep in mind that you are only as strong as the people you rely on and you will be stronger still. Self-reliance is a good thing, but *other*-reliance is essential. And let yourself be that *other* for others. After all, no man is an island. No matter how good we are at our jobs, no matter how smart or intuitive we are, some things will forever be out of our control. Know that sooner or later you'll need help and it will have to come from somewhere, so you might as well go looking for it.

THREE
The Price Is Right

Success to me is having ten honeydew melons,
and eating only the top half of each one.
—Barbra Streisand

One of my mother's favorite sayings has always been "The train never gets to the station." As a kid, I had no idea what she meant by it. I used to think maybe she just didn't like trains or trust the transit schedule, but as I got older, I took her point. She meant for me and my sisters to enjoy the ride, wherever we were going. Whatever our goals, it wouldn't do to reach for them unless we got something out of the reaching—because in the end you might never get to your destination, or you might find a better, more interesting stop along the way.

Yes, the reaching is key, but so too is the goal—and I am determined to get where I'm going and to enjoy the ride, both. It's a mind-set that mixes high expectations with a worthy pursuit, and I can't see the one without the other. For me, when I wake up in the morning and head off to work, I have to be excited about what I'm doing. I have to be juiced. Otherwise, what's the point? There are millions of people in this country just going through the motions, hating what they do and muscling their way through each day. Even today I look on at folks like that and think they're never going to be successful, because they're never going to be willing to go that extra mile to do what needs to get done. Their heart's not in it, and if your heart's not in it, you're nowhere.

But let me get back to my mother's train analogy and the joy in the reaching. I reached next to the campus of Bradley University in Peoria, Illinois, still thinking I'd be a lawyer and still charged with the idea of making money and creating value. My plan was to major in criminology, and I stuck to it, even though my focus was more on my sideline business activities than on my classes. My grades were strong enough, but my head was elsewhere. All along, I kept swapping out cars, running through an awesome Jeep CJ7, a Jeep Wrangler Sahara, an IROC Convertible, a Toyota 4Runner . . . each time netting enough money to keep me in books and pizza and a new car to keep me roadworthy. The money was significant because Bradley was something of a stretch for my parents—especially with me as the fourth Rancic child in pursuit of a college degree. Mostly, though, it was something of a stretch for me too. I supplemented my parents' tuition contribution in what ways I could, but I was on my own for room and board and any social expenses. For once, my focus on money had as much to do with need as greed, and I wasn't sure that I liked having my hand out.

Despite my extracurricular distractions, I did reasonably well that first year because I had a clear goal in mind

> There are no secrets to success but working harder than the guy next to you, thinking smarter than the guy next to you, and wanting it just a little more than the guy next to you.

and knew that even a slight misstep in my grades could cost me a shot at a top law school. I was determined and driven, making money and headway and not really taking my mother's advice to heart because my emphasis, I'll admit, was more on the goal than the journey. I still got a special charge out of every car deal, but my courses didn't offer the excitement or the challenge I'd thought they might.

It took a while, but I finally realized I was more interested in *being* a lawyer than I was in actually *becoming* a lawyer, and college is all about becoming, isn't it? Anyway, that's what I'd been led to believe, and it takes me back to my mother's train analogy and ahead to the ways I've tried to live my life ever since. In school, I found myself focusing more and more on life outside the classroom, checking out cars and girls and parties. I continued to pull good grades, but my head was all over the place, and soon enough it would be back home in Chicago. Some time during my freshman year, my dad took a teaching job at Loyola University in downtown Chicago, so I switched gears before my sophomore year and enrolled there, where children of faculty enjoyed free tuition and where I could continue studying criminology. The savings were a big deal to my parents, who by then had two graduate school tuitions to worry about, and a boon to me personally because I wouldn't have to take out any additional student loans. I'd still have some considerable expenses, such as books and room and board, but the tuition credit was a great benefit. And to top it all off, I thought the change of scenery would do me good.

And it did. I made a bunch of great new friends and had a chance to reconnect with some of my childhood buddies who had remained in the area. In the reshuffling I was forced to face one of the first crucial decisions of my adult life: what to do about a summer job. Okay, maybe *crucial* is too strong a word in this case, but at the time it loomed as a big deal. All around me, friends were accepting low-paying entry-level jobs in their fields of interest, or volunteer internships just to get their foot in some door, or minimum wage jobs in maintenance or child care or fast food. They were doing what they had to do, what everyone else was doing, while I couldn't seem to push myself forward. There wasn't a whole lot out there to get me pumped about working, especially now that I had come to place a high value on my time from my string of successful car deals.

One of my first thoughts, actually, was to try to make a full-time go of things in the used-car market, to have several deals brewing at a time, but I talked myself out of this notion when I realized I'd have to overextend myself to make it work. Restoring one car at a time, I could at least justify the cost of my investment by driving the car until I found an opportunity to sell it, but that was about all I could handle. I didn't have the deep pockets or the line of credit to reasonably absorb any kind of inventory. Plus, I didn't think I had the time.

But these car deals did set me straight on what I wanted out of a summer job. Or at least what I *didn't* want. I didn't want to sit behind a desk or stand watch for a small hourly wage while someone else got rich off my efforts. I'd done just that during the school year in a part-time gig at FAO Schwarz, the giant toy store, where I worked in undercover security. It was my job to catch shoplifters, which sounds a whole lot more exciting than it actually was, but I kept at it because the hours were flexible and the store was not far from campus. And on paper at least, the job offered a ground-floor view of criminal law, which at that point was still a long-term goal of mine.

Try as I might, I just couldn't see myself working store security indoors for an entire summer. The prospect seemed to be about as exciting as watching paint dry. And as I recall, FAO Schwarz wouldn't even let its part-time employees work full-time hours, because then they'd have to start paying us overtime and providing certain other benefits and that wasn't about to happen. It was just as well. I'd come to value my time too much to sell myself short at four dollars an hour. It was one thing to work for so little during the school year, when my schedule was tight and my options few and the extra money came in handy. But over the summer I wanted to come and go as I pleased, make good money, and possibly learn a thing or two in the bargain, and if it came bundled together with the chance to meet girls and hang out in the sun, so much the better.

It's never too early to make the most out of not much at all.

With these things in mind, my best friend Jerry Agema and I came up with a plan. It was a brainstorm wrapped inside another no-brainer. Jerry and I had gone to high school together, and he was off at Northern Illinois, worrying about his own summer plans, so we decided to start a business washing and waxing boats. We backed into this plan, really. Jerry's father was the CFO of the Tribune Company, a very smart, very successful guy, and his family had a vacation house up in New Buffalo, Michigan, a summer resort town about an hour north of Chicago. It's like the Hamptons of the Midwest, and our first thought had been to locate our business there, right on the water. I'd been to visit a bunch of times, and the thought of spending our summer there was argument enough in favor of launching the business. In fact we settled on our *base* of operations before we figured out our operations. We didn't scratch our heads and think, Okay, what can we do to earn some decent money? We thought, Okay, what can we do to earn some decent money *in New Buffalo?* There's a difference, and I mention it here for the way it reinforces the importance of a focused approach. It's not enough to hope for a bright idea; you have to think with a goal in mind and work backwards. Ask yourself, "How do I get there from here?" and you're on your way.

Once we hit on the idea, we were all over it; we'd have a place to stay, a built-in clientele, and virtually no overhead outside of some wax, some towels, and some buffers. Plus nobody in New Buffalo was offering the same type of service. There was a marina in town that washed and waxed, but clients had to bring their boats to the shop, whereas we were planning to go to the boat. There were other marinas too, up and down the shore, but nobody offered quite this type of service, so we were liking the fact that we would have the marketplace essentially to ourselves.

> If you fall in lockstep with everyone else, you'll never get ahead.

We called ourselves Elite Boat Wash and Wax, and our goal was in our name. We aimed to attract New Buffalo's high-end boaters—those guys with the fifty-, sixty-, eighty-foot cruisers who came to town on the weekends with boatloads of money and who didn't have the time or the inclination to do the job themselves. We'd get to be outdoors on the water all summer long. We'd work hard, set our own hours, take on only as much work as we felt we could handle, expand the business to meet demand if we determined it was in our best interests, and generally have ourselves a blast.

In some respects, what we had in mind was similar to a lawn-mowing or a pool-cleaning business—traditional summer jobs for enterprising college kids looking to strike out on their own. The real difference between our job and the others lay in what we could charge our customers and in how we might grow or market our efforts. We weren't setting out to create busywork for ourselves or to earn money by doing the chores we used to reject as kids; we were hoping to build a business.

Our business plan was simple: offer first-class service at first-class prices to a potential customer base accustomed to nothing less than the very best. We'd charge $400 for a complete wash and wax, thinking it would take the two of us half a day to complete the job and that we would need to land only a few such gigs a week to make the effort a success. Before establishing the price, we called around to some marinas and boat owners to price the market and then rounded everyone's best guess up to the nearest $100. This, we thought, was a killer move. Instead of valuing our time along a minimum wage model, we priced our service at the edge of what we thought our customers would bear. If we misread the market—that is, if customers were reluctant to throw in with us on price alone—we could always negotiate downward or offer incentive deals built on volume, or even go back to the drawing board and come up with a new fee structure.

We also offered a weekly wash service for $30 or $40 per boat per week, depending on the size of the boat, thinking we could open up a whole other segment of the market at this lower price point and fill in the downtime between our big jobs with this lesser work. The deal was, if you signed on for an entire summer's worth of service, we'd wash the boat during the week and have the thing looking spit-shined and lake-worthy by Friday afternoon, when most folks tended to come to town for the weekend. Or you could contract with us on a one-time basis for a simple wash. In addition, there were all kinds of other one-time services we provided, such as cleaning out a water line, staining deck furniture, or doing whatever our customers needed done. Hell, we would have stocked their kitchens for them if they made it worth our while.

The business took off. It was more of a service, really, than a bricks-and-mortar establishment, but whatever you called it, we were all over it. We had our wash and wax kits and we were good to go. We lined up a number of clients at the front end of the season, hoping other clients would follow through positive word of mouth and thoughtful promotion. We fielded phone calls and tracked our billing and expenses from Jerry's lake house, but for the most part we were out on our clients' boats, working like crazy. In the beginning, we got a lot of referrals through Jerry's dad, and people Jerry and his family already knew in New Buffalo, and the plan was to do such a kick-ass job with these clients that our name would get around. The amazing fact was that no one else was doing quite the same thing, which was just what we expected, so we really did have a corner on the market. The key would come in identifying that market for the good people of New Buffalo—that is, convincing them they needed a service such as ours and getting them to pay for it and to wonder how they'd gotten along without us for all of their boat-owning lives.

Our target customers were successful, hardworking people, and they meant to enjoy their summer weekends, not to swab their own decks, and as soon as Jerry and I were there, folks wanted in. We did a great job and came across as super-hungry and anxious to please, and folks seemed to want to do business with us, which we took as a tribute to our work ethic as much as a nod to our winning concept. The weekly washes were a big hit because of their low price point, but surprisingly the full wax treatment wasn't as tough a sell as we thought it might be. We even had a few customers who scheduled a wax job every month, so by the time that first Memorial Day rolled around Jerry and I had more than enough work.

That first summer, we built our business up to about thirty weekly washes, mostly through referrals, with a full wash and wax scheduled several times each week. Sometimes we'd slot in a second complete job on the same day, and there were even times mid-week that we'd tackle a third, working well into the night. The money was too good to pass up, and yet there was plenty of time to loaf and hang out with girls, one of the fringe bene-fits. We worked seven days a week—or five or six, depending on the weather and our busy social schedules. Another fringe benefit: we managed to water-ski every single day, weather permitting, so there was balance, and for the first time in my working life I began to recognize quality of life as an essential line in my personal ledger.

Once we figured out what we were doing, it took about thirty to forty minutes to complete a standard boat wash, with the two of us working together double-time. We tried to be as efficient as possible, and one of the best efficiencies,

> **S**ometimes going that extra yard simply means you're willing to take on a job no one else wants or has thought of doing.

we discovered, was to kill ourselves with hard work. The faster and smarter we worked, the more we accomplished, and the more we accomplished, the more business we could take on. We established a route and a routine, working one end of the marina each day to cut down on time lost hauling our butts to each rig. Some customers insisted on having their boats washed immediately before the weekend, on Thursday or Friday, and we tried to accommodate—provided they paid extra for the extra service. Ideally we'd do a full wash and wax in the morning and a half-dozen washes in the afternoon and call it a day. We'd get our skiing in first thing, when the water was still and conditions were ideal, or we'd catch a sunset run if it was shaping up to be a nice night. Or if there was something cool happening at the beach or a party we felt we absolutely *had* to attend, we'd double up on our stops for a couple of days until we had everything covered.

Focus on opportunities you'll enjoy pursuing. Avoid situations you know you'll come to dread.

Conservatively, we were taking in about $1,500 to $2,000 per week total, although some weeks—at the height of the summer, going full throttle—we could make almost twice that amount, and as we counted our receipts we counted ourselves fortunate. We were young and fairly loaded with cash and having the time of our lives. All was right with our little worlds. I can still picture us on one of our clients' boats late one summer afternoon, kicking back after a hard day's work on a forty-five-foot Cigarette boat, and just then it was the stuff of my dreams—sleek, stylin', and just about the coolest thing on the water. Whenever I wished myself into this type of lifestyle, I never saw myself with one of those great cruiser yachts. At nineteen years old, I saw myself throwing down the hammer on one of these slick Cigarette boats, pushing the limits out on the open water. That to me was the picture of success. A boat like that probably ran a couple hundred thousand, easy, and it had my name on it. Really. This particular boat was christened *Billy the Kid*, an unavoidable childhood nickname that I was proud to wear here, so Jerry and I posed for pictures and imagined ourselves big-city playboys breezing into town in search of good times and fast company.

I wasn't quite there yet, but in my head I had arrived.

I suppose it wasn't the healthiest thing in the world, to envy the wealth of our customers and imagine ourselves into their lives (and onto their boats!), and it certainly wasn't the most professional, but to quite literally rub up against these totems of success and achievement, day in and day out, was an intoxicating thrill. Let me tell you, being on these killer boats all summer long was a powerful lure, the carrot to end all carrots. It was also a great equalizer, because it taught me that you didn't have to be a rocket scientist or a Harvard Business School graduate or any other kind of genius to make a big success of yourself. I'd talk to our clients and come away thinking, Well, *this* one's not that bright. Or I'd be suitably unimpressed by an exchange and wonder how in the world *that* guy made all that money. Really, a lot of these people didn't seem to have a whole lot going on upstairs, with no more or less on the ball than anybody else I was coming into contact with; their wealth and accomplishments in no way matched their personalities, and Jerry and I came away thinking that if they could achieve this kind of lifestyle, then it was within our reach as well. It was an important lesson, taught to us by a bunch of folks who didn't seem to have a clue. We started out feeling a little intimidated by our clients and ended up convinced we fit right in; the transformation was liberating. It left us thinking we could do anything—and that we should probably get to it.

By the Fourth of July weekend, Elite Boat Wash and Wax was really cranking, to where some of our clients who kept boats back in Chicago started to ask us if we could offer the same service there—to which we could only reply in the affirmative. The lesson here, learned by the seat of our pants, was never to turn down work; our guts told us to say yes to everything and figure out how to keep our end of the bargain later. And that's just what we did. I hired a friend of mine to work the same deal out of the Belmont Harbor area downtown, and she was able to handle the work on her own. Once a week, I'd make a run back home to pick up our checks, troubleshoot whatever problems might have come up during the week, and restock my friend with supplies, and then I'd hustle back up to New Buffalo to service our clients there.

> **K**eep learning—and always remember there is no end to possibility.

For our second summer on the water, Jerry and I were looking to make some improvements to our operation. We had a successful formula, but we were determined to build on that success, and to that end we thought we'd kick off our season with a marketing plan. We'd invested some of the previous summer's profits into some equipment we felt would make us more efficient and proficient on the job, which in turn left us thinking we could handle a bigger workload, so we set about designing an elaborate flyer to showcase our wares and help grow our business. We used thick black lettering on eye-catching fluorescent orange paper and set about canvassing the harbor one midweek afternoon before the Memorial Day weekend, which traditionally started New Buffalo's summer season. We placed the flyers on every boat we could find, wherever we thought it might catch the owners' attention—in the cabins, on the windshield glass, affixed neatly to the hull—and then we went back to Jerry's place and waited for the phone to ring.

Well, we should have consulted a weather report because those flyers nearly came back to bite us in a big way. Right after we finished distributing them, a torrential rain bucketed down on the region, and when the skies finally cleared, Jerry and I wandered down to the harbor to take in the scene—and, as it turned out, to assess the damage. It seemed that the ink on our flyers had mixed with the fluorescent orange from the paper to leave all kinds of weird and wild stains on almost every boat we had "marketed." The damn flyers had bled all over these million-dollar boats. Jerry and I were screwed. What had only a couple hours earlier seemed like a promising marketing campaign was now looking like a disaster, and we scrambled to regroup. I immediately called a cousin of mine who was in his first year of law school, which despite our first-summer success was still the best legal counsel we could afford, to assess what our exposure might be if one of these boat owners turned out to mind that we had defaced his property.

It almost didn't matter what the answer was on the exposure question, because what was at risk here was our hard-won reputation and not our liability; really, the only thing to do was make things right, and the only way to do that was to scrub each and every boat until it shined like new. Trouble was, as bad luck would have it, a simple scrubbing wasn't about to do the trick, because these were tough, stubborn stains. There was just the two of us, and we had pretty much blanketed that harbor, so we had to double-time it in order to undo the damage before the holiday weekend. We climbed aboard boat after boat and scrubbed and buffed and made those yachts look like new. Ended up working a few nights until one or two in the morning, just to get through it, and I realize now we probably shouldn't have even been on those yachts in the first place. I don't think we even thought about this, because it never occurred to us that anyone would see what we were up to and think to press trespassing charges. We were just hardworking college kids who'd made an honest mistake and caused some cosmetic damage to some expensive vessels, and we were simply trying to make repairs.

Do the right thing, even if there's no one around to take note.

We wound up walking off the pier after finishing our damage control on the very last boat just as one of our customers was stepping onto the pier to board his own vessel, so we really cut it close, and Jerry and I breathed an exaggerated sigh as this guy passed. But word got around about what had happened. It's a small town, New Buffalo, and people talk, and folks had seen us scrubbing away the ink and dye from all those boats, and it made an impression. The way the story got passed around from one townsperson to the next left the two of us looking resourceful and reliable and willing to do whatever it took to make things right. Sure we'd screwed up big-time, but we came away from it looking golden—and in the end the mishap probably won us a bunch of customers and earned us a mess of goodwill.

We had a great run with Elite Boat Wash and Wax those two college summers, but it couldn't last forever. Graduation loomed, and Jerry and I had plans. Ultimately it was a seasonal business—perfect for college kids looking to work outdoors and pile on some cash, but probably without the growth potential we were looking for in our careers. My one regret is that we didn't think to sell the business before we skipped town after that second summer, because I look back now and think we really did manage to create a valuable enterprise. Out of nothing, we had built a strong, loyal customer base, with two years of credit and payment history. We created a market where none had existed, providing a service no one else had thought to offer. We earned a solid reputation, one that was enhanced in that second summer by our willingness to clean all those boats. We even had a satellite operation being run out of Belmont Harbor in Chicago, which certainly suggested some kind of blueprint at work here. Clearly, Jerry and I *were* the business; without our sweat and effort, we had nothing. But there were tangible assets to what we had built.

Problem was, it never occurred to either one of us to sell it. We were too stupid or too focused on our last year of college or too frantic over what we would do after graduation. In our thinking, the business had run its course. It had made us a ton of money and afforded us two great summers, and the good people of New Buffalo would have to go back to washing and waxing their own boats—or find other enterprising college kids to overcharge them for the privilege of doing it for them.

By the following summer, we would be on to bigger and better things. Anyway, that was the plan.

Lessons Learned
ON STRATEGY

BE THE BEE Consider the flight of the bumblebee. According to all reasonable laws of physics, the bumblebee is not meant to fly. Its wing-to-weight ratio should prohibit it from ever getting off the ground. But nobody told the bee, and the bee flies. Be the bee. Indeed, be whatever it is folks least expect, and do whatever it takes to get a thing done.

BREAK FROM THE PACK If you fall in lockstep with everyone else, you'll never get ahead. Think of every great innovation or initiative and note that it likely succeeded in direct relation to how much it strayed from the norm. No one ever got rich going through the same motions as their competitors. Avis didn't build a brand with the motto "We try pretty much just as hard as the other guys." Beg to differ, accentuate those differences, and hope to find your niche in the space that separates you from the fold.

SEPARATE YOUR EXPECTATIONS FROM YOUR SHORTCOMINGS Many successful people are oblivious to their weaknesses (and there are even some who are just plain oblivious), but the individual who powers through his or her failings or works to rise above them is the one who knows true and lasting success. In grammar school, when faced with the fear of dangling participles and split infinitives, I avoided writing sentences that didn't *sound* right. I wrote around the problem without really solving it or learning the material. In the world of business there's no avoiding the problem. You can cross your fingers and hope for the best, but the problems will eventually find you. Count on it. The only way to ensure a successful outcome is to cover all the bases. Learn the material. Anticipate the problem. Know your stuff. Know your boss's stuff. Know your competitor's stuff.

GO ABOVE AND BEYOND If everyone is willing and able to perform the same service, you'll never make any money. If no one is willing or able, there's probably a reason—but there's also an opportunity.

MAKE EACH DAY COUNT—TWICE Work two days every day. Seven in the morning until noon, and then again from noon to seven in the evening. Work through lunch. Get more done than anyone else. Know that when you're sitting on your hands or twiddling your thumbs, someone else is pushing the envelope and busting his butt. I've borrowed the two-a-day concept from some of the most demanding college coaches in the country, who put their players through double workouts in order to maximize their training in a minimum time frame. Splitting the day into two distinct sessions gives you a psychological edge first thing in the morning. It can be an intimidating thing, to wonder how you'll ever reach the end of the day. Break it down and go far.

UNDERPROMISE AND OVERDELIVER The line that you get only one chance to make a first impression has been repeated endlessly, but it resonates in the marketplace because most customers will give you only one try to make a sale. Most bosses will give you only one look before sizing you up. Most coworkers will write you off the first time you drop the ball. And most team leaders will look to someone else if you failed to execute the first time around. If you're risking your time and money and reputation on an entrepreneurial idea, make double sure that your product and service are better than the competition. Make sure you've thought of every contingency. If you're caught short at the outset and intend to bridge the gap as you develop, your customers and your in-house supporters will be long gone by the time you get your act together.

STAY QUICK ON YOUR FEET Your level of success in business will directly correlate with your ability to shift gears and respond to changing market conditions. Shit happens, and you have to be prepared to deal with it, respond to it, and move on. Agility and adaptability are key. Shift on the fly. If an approach proves ineffective the first time out, it's a miscalculation; if that same approach doesn't work on a second try, it's poor leadership.

TAKE PRIDE IN YOUR WORK Own your efforts and your ideas. As much as anything else, they're the hard currency of the workplace. But even more important is the stamp you put on everything you do. In a service business, customers buy people. Sell your enthusiasm, your dedication, and your willingness to make things right.

GET A GOOD NIGHT'S SLEEP Whenever and wherever possible. You never know what the next day might bring.

FOUR
Business as Usual

He was a self-made man who owed
his lack of success to nobody.

–Joseph Heller

O ne of the great fringe benefits of my Elite Boat Wash
and Wax experience was that it taught me to value
my time in a whole new way—and this was a lesson
I'd carry going forward. Too often we make our professional
choices based on what we perceive as our financial needs instead of on what we think our time is actually worth, so I
tried to rethink the equation as I looked ahead to what I
might do next.

At this point, after running my own business and setting
my own terms, the concept of working for someone else at a
low hourly wage held no appeal. Worse, it seemed a step
backward. Even an entry-level salaried position, starting in
the same $20,000 range where most of my buddies seemed to
be falling, worked out to less than $10 an hour over the
course of a full year, full-time, and I just couldn't see logging
that kind of load for that kind of money. I wasn't opposed to
hard work, but I was dead set against low pay. I'd been
spoiled, really, by the $400 Jerry and I were able to charge
for the half a day it took to do a complete wax and wash, the

good money we could make in a good week, so as college wound down I held out for something more.

Law school was still a fallback option, but my interest in trying cases seemed to have faded, and even if it reappeared, I wanted to get some real-world experience before signing on for another three years of school. After graduation I fumbled about for a bit, considering my next move. I really did make the statement that I wouldn't get out of bed for less than $50,000 a year, and I really did mean to stick to it. Of course I didn't set that figure out there and expect some voodoo magic to win me a job at that salary; I went out and looked for it, with every intention of working hard at it, but the gods of entry-level employment seemed to be looking the other way at the time.

> If you sell yourself short, you'll never come out ahead.

In any case, I'd run some scenarios in my head and come back thinking $1,000 a week seemed about right for someone of my limited experience and unlimited potential. I felt I needed to put a number on it. I may have been brash and cocky, but I decided that $50,000 was what my time was worth, and I wouldn't shortchange myself unless there was some other compelling piece to the deal.

My friends all thought I was nuts. My parents, too. They couldn't understand how it was that everyone else was landing these seemingly important jobs with big-time companies, while I had yet to find anything, and after a while even I began to question the wisdom of my position. I mean, my friends were all *working*. They were out there striving, hoping to make a difference, while I was just holding out. They may have settled for jobs they didn't particularly love, at salaries they didn't particularly care for, but at least they were gaining valuable experience, moving forward, getting about the business of a career.

Don't get me wrong, I wasn't just lying about during this time, waiting for the phone to ring. I was doing what I could to make something happen, even though not a whole lot was happening. I was going on interviews, sending out résumés and scouring the newspapers for out-of-the-way opportunities . . . but nothing appeared to be coming out of my efforts, not even the chance to fetch coffee or dry-cleaning for some mid-level suit. And certainly no one was knocking down my door trying to give me $1,000 a week.

When that commodity metals sales job surfaced, then, I talked myself into believing the commission setup would help me meet my goals and leave me essentially free to establish my own hours, develop my own style, and operate with some autonomy. But the more I worked that job, the more I realized I could never get and keep ahead pushing someone else's product. I learned a lot on that job, and I became a good, hustling salesman. I'd sold myself as such going in, and convinced the guy doing the hiring that I could cover my territory with a youthful exuberance not seen on his current sales force. I lived up to my own billing before long, picking up a thing or two about letting the product speak for itself, packaging incentives into a purchase, and pushing a customer toward closing without letting on that I was pushing. I tried to discover something in both every rejection and every successful sale—and something about myself in the bargain.

Still, after seeing how management tossed that company lifer when his contract got too big to justify, I realized I could never get any kind of job security, no matter how successful I was as a salesperson, so I started looking for a way to free myself from my paycheck and the whims of my employers. I set about playing to my strengths as I cast about for an opportunity that might appeal to my emerging entrepreneurial sensibilities. And just what were my strengths, at twenty-four, with virtually no professional experience? Well, I thought I was a good salesman, and expected that the tools I'd used to sell cars and boat-cleaning services and commodity metals would serve me well in any endeavor. I was creative, aggressive, and relatively fearless . . . good things, all, if you mean to make a strong presentation. I had a good work ethic. It might not come across, with my stating how unappealing it was to work long hours for little return, but I could put in the time if I had a stake in what I was doing—if what I was doing *mattered* in almost any sense of the word. And I've since realized that I had particularly strong marketing skills, although I didn't recognize them at the time as marketing skills. Back then, I just thought of myself as a hustler. Not in a pejorative sense, but in a good way. I was young, energetic, and willing to roll up my sleeves to get the job done, as long as there was some kind of reward for my extra efforts.

That's what it always came down to, in my estimation, the payday at the end of the effort. If I couldn't see the upside, I couldn't be bothered, and as soon as I couldn't see the upside in that metals job I started looking elsewhere. I let it be known around the office that I had one foot out the door, and soon enough my salesman pals were on me about it bigtime. They caught me looking at "Investors Needed" and "Partners Wanted" opportunities in the back of the newspaper, and razzed me about it. They heard me talking about franchise opportunities. I actually looked closely at a Subway franchise deal before rejecting it on a worst-case scenario basis. I discovered early on, running the boat washing and waxing business, that if you factor in the worst-case scenarios and still come up with an effective business plan you're way ahead of the game. In the case of the Subway shop, I realized that as often as not, someone would call in sick or we'd be short-staffed and I'd have to work the line making sandwiches myself.

Now, as much as I liked the idea of making money, that's how much I didn't like the idea of making sandwiches. Nothing against the folks who make this choice for themselves, but I just did not see myself slathering mayonnaise on someone's twelve-inch sandwich—baking someone else's daily bread in order to earn mine, so to speak. The more I looked at this Subway franchise, the more I realized I'd be buying myself a job instead of a career. That's how I broke it down, and it was essentially the same deal with every franchise I considered. As I said, if you look at these things from a Murphy's Law perspective, it was not a pretty picture. I'd be a slave to whatever enterprise I was buying into, and the prospect wasn't all that appealing.

Don't misunderstand, I'm not opposed to hard work. I love to work. I live for it, actually, but the work has got to be interesting to get me going. I've got to love what I do. Busywork holds no appeal. I want to lead and motivate, not follow and be intimidated. Plus, there needs to be opportunities for creativity, innovation, and gamesmanship, and I knew I'd never find these things on the assembly line behind the counter at Subway. So I continued my search.

As I looked around the Chicago area for opportunities, I started to think of myself as an entrepreneur. I'd run my own successful summer business and found ways to make money out of no money at all, but I'd never used that word *entrepreneur* to describe myself, and when one of the other metals salesmen pinned it on me one afternoon at the health club I gave it some thought. He meant it as a good-natured rib— as in "Hey Rancic, you're a regular *entrepreneur*," almost like it was a dirty word—but I chose to take it as a compliment and guessed that there were two different mind-sets in the world of business.

> **B**uild your dreams on a strong foundation.

I grabbed at the label as if it was a lifeline, and in truth, it was. As an entrepreneur, I gave myself the freedom to shake things up, to reinvent each task. Even at this commodity metals company, I was an entrepreneur working under a corporate umbrella, and I realize now that's a distinction that's lost on most of us. Yes, it's possible to be innovative and entrepreneurial on someone else's dime, and those who survive and thrive in the corporate workplace often demonstrate these traits every day. Those who flounder will look ahead to an endless string of more of the same. I told myself there'd be no "same old, same old" in my workaday world. No one day would be quite like another, and I would be up to every challenge. I really psyched myself into this way of thinking, and as I did, I realized I'd been thinking this way all along. There was no need for any kind of internal hard sell. This was what I was, an entrepreneur; it was part of my makeup, and now that my buddies at work had put a label on me I was all over it. Of course, in reality I was still just a salesman, with no real enterprise to validate my position, but I was determined to change that. And soon.

I put the word out that I was open to anything, and soon

enough the word came back with a couple of prospects. A buddy of mine from school, Kyle Koch, called about a bar he knew that was for sale. At this point I had hooked up with another buddy named John Cawley, who was finishing up his MBA and looking for a situation to call his own. John was a good numbers guy and I thought his talents would mesh with my sales and marketing instincts. It occurred to each of us we might increase our opportunities exponentially if we threw our lot in together—either on this bar prospect or on some other shot.

I kicked it around for a bit and thought, Okay, I can own a bar. That could be cool. I'd still have to work the line from time to time—mixing drinks, washing glasses—but it wouldn't be the same kind of drudgery as making sandwiches. I'd be like Sam Malone on *Cheers*, hanging out with interesting people, making each day a kind of party and making good money in the bargain.

We went out to take a look at the place, though, and it turned out to be a bondage bar. We should have figured it out just from the name: Aftermath. Not exactly the Pig 'N Whistle or the Blarney Stone, eh? It would have been funny if it wasn't so frustrating. John had had no idea, either, but as long as we were there, we took a look around. They had a rack, a dungeon, all kinds of whips and chains, and whatever else it is you tend to find in bondage bars; it clearly wasn't the opportunity we'd thought it might be. We didn't know much about the bar business, and we knew even less about the bondage bar business, but we knew that whatever business we chose to pursue, we most likely wouldn't be able to afford real employees and would have to enlist our parents, our siblings, and whoever else we could rope into the deal. It would have to be a real ground-floor operation, and I just couldn't see asking our mothers to work the cat-o'-nine-tails, so we moved on.

Be realistic.

Another viable prospect surfaced with a used sporting goods store, but here again the worst-case scenario put me off. The business made sense and the start-up costs were relatively low, but I just couldn't see myself chasing yard sales and consignment shops, haggling on a price for some kid's old baseball glove. I've since seen a couple of small chains of used sporting goods stores turn up in different markets around the country, and in retrospect I could have done fairly well with this business model, but I wanted to love waking up in the morning to go to work and I couldn't see loving the bats and balls of this one.

Finally, nine months into my commodity metals job and about three or four months into my start-up search, a light-bulb flashed over my head. That's how it happens sometimes, and all that's needed is to recognize the bright idea when it lights up in your head. In this case, it wasn't even my own bright idea to start; it was someone else's, mixed with my own new notion, which presumably added to the wattage. I was sitting with John Cawley in a café in downtown Chicago. We were kicking around all these different opportunities, spitballing, trying to find something we could grab onto that might pull us from our routines. Over the course of our running around, looking at everything and anything, we'd come across some guys who'd launched a fairly successful mail-order business selling microbrewery and boutique beers on a subscription basis. They were from Chicago and called their company Beers Across America. For a while they had some success selling monthly or annual memberships through radio and print advertising in targeted markets. I'd always liked the simplicity of their concept, their launch, and their ongoing efforts.

It was one of those businesses that left people like me wondering, Hey, why didn't I think of that? The concept, for those of you who never gave or received one of these memberships or came across one of their ads, was to broker the sale of hard-to-find regional beers as a gift item. For a set fee, customers could order a six-pack of an award-winning beer each month, for anywhere from three months to a year—for themselves or for a gift. Or they could order two or more six-packs each month. Beers Across America would select the beers, cut special deals with each brewery, and handle the shipping, and they'd collect the money from their customers up front to fund their operation.

In all, a masterstroke of a mail-order concept, and they'd been in the back of my mind because of their radio spots and because we knew each other and because every time I sipped some specialty beer I invariably thought of them. It was a boom time for microbreweries and high-end beers, and theirs was really a solid concept; they'd done a great job promoting it and creating a niche market where none had existed before. John and I were pulling out our hair trying to come up with something that would work as well for us.

So that's a little bit of the back story to this lightbulb-over-the-head moment. The front story was this: four well-dressed Europeans sat down at a table across from us at the café. One by one they lit up cigars. They didn't just light the things; they took them out and sniffed them and studied them and talked about them. This was back when you could still light up a stogie in most pubs and cafés, so the scene itself wasn't anything out of the ordinary. What was extraordinary about this particular scene, at just this moment, was what the cigars came to represent in my thinking. Despite whatever Sigmund Freud had to say on the matter, I realize that sometimes a cigar is just a cigar, but here it was somewhat more. It was a signal of achievement, a status symbol, a quiet, hard-won indulgence. It was all these things and more, and as these men considered their cigars, I considered this.

I gestured for John to look over at their table and said, "Cigars Around the World," and in that one instant and in that one simple phrase we both knew we were onto something—and that what we were onto would be much the same as our beer-peddling friends.

> When all else fails, try something completely different.

With cigars, we thought we could go the beer business one or two better. Our shipping and packaging costs would be far less (and we wouldn't have to worry about handling all of those glass bottles!). Our warehouse needs would also be far less intimidating, because a package of, say, five premium cigars takes up a whole lot less room than a couple of six-packs, which would have been a comparably priced order. Most important, though, was the great vibe we were getting about cigars and their place on our social landscape. Cigar magazines were starting to appear on newsstands—usually with an A-list celebrity on the cover singing the praises of his or her favorite blend. In many ways, the cigar scene mirrored the trend with microbreweries and high-end beers. Upscale cigar bars and smoking rooms were starting to turn up in some of our trendiest urban markets—although, surprisingly, I was not yet aware of any that had opened in

Chicago. Cigars as the vice/habit/hobby of choice among young urban professionals seemed about to break in a big way, and we had pretty much stumbled onto a path to some serious money.

Right there in the café, we developed our business strategy. For $24.95 per month, customers would get five different premium hand-rolled cigars, a newsletter, and a cigar cutter, all in a smart, stay-fresh package. We had no idea what these premium cigars would *really* cost, but the price point seemed about right. We'd been in enough nice restaurants and country clubs and hotel bars to know that a single fresh cigar rarely sells for less than a couple of bucks, so cigar smokers were conditioned to this kind of pricing. Plus, we would price in incentives to get people to order for more than one month—buy six months, get one month free; buy twelve months, get two months free; that sort of thing. And we would encourage customers to buy multi-month memberships as gifts, perfect for Father's Day, Christmas, birthdays, and so on.

The more we thought about it, the more we liked the idea of a mail-order cigar business, so we continued to weigh its advantages:

- It was doable, something we felt we could handle with our relatively limited experience.
- It was sellable. We'd be creating value as we built our business, to where an investor might spark to our customer base or our increasingly recognizable brand.
- It highlighted a growing national phenomenon, popularized by some of our leading celebrities.
- It appealed to our shared sense of leisure and accomplishment and reasonable excess.

- There was an extremely low barrier of entry. Indeed, we could launch with a simple leafleting campaign and purchase inventory only to fill our first orders, on a just-in-time basis.
- It traded on an established marketing strategy and thus would allow us to concentrate our efforts on promoting the product instead of the club membership concept.
- We could operate out of John's apartment for a while, and hit the ground running without having to hire anyone else.
- We weren't creating a "retail jail," a storefront outlet or a restaurant, bar, or other cash business where we would essentially be hostages to our hours of operation.
- Perhaps most significant, it looked like a whole lot of fun, to be out there peddling a high-end, high-trend product like fine cigars, to high-flying young professionals like ourselves.

This last was something we could get excited about, and I knew enough to realize it would be far easier to sell from enthusiasm than from indifference. About the only negative we could pinpoint was that the Cigars Around the World concept was so simple it could easily be pirated by a competitor, but we figured we'd have a running start and reminded ourselves that nobody remembers the *second* team of astronauts to walk on the moon. It's the pioneers who get all the credit—and, we hoped, the bulk of the business.

The real beauty of our business model was we wouldn't need any kind of inventory to start taking orders. We could work it so that we'd send out a gift or acknowledgment card immediately upon taking the order, which we wouldn't start filling until the following month. It was actually a sweet setup, given our financial constraints, and the more we kicked the idea around, the more we liked it.

The only real negative was that neither of us knew a thing about cigars. That hadn't stopped me from making some noise in the commodity metals business, and it hadn't stopped John in his previous hustles, and we weren't about to let it stop us here. Like I said, I was a quick study. I was also fiercely determined to make this thing work, even if it meant finding my way into Cuba and learning from the best in the business how to roll the damn things myself.

Almost immediately, I gave notice at the commodity metals company, and I took some grief from the guys for leaving to go it alone. I left on good terms, and my boss wished me well, but he let me know that he thought I was doomed to fail. He even told me I could come back and claim my old job if things didn't work out, which was decent of him.

I was still only twenty-four years old and I figured, What the hell did I have to lose? A job I liked only for the money? A too-easy routine? Some budding friendships with guys twice my age, all of whom had been phoning it in for most of their working lives, waiting for the day when they too could be canned for no good reason? Really, there wasn't a whole lot at stake here, and if I stood pat and did nothing but beat the pavement for the next thirty years, I might still be out on my ass, even if I turned out to be the best salesman the company had ever seen. That was the simple truth and the best reason I could find for striking out on my own.

We put together some seed money—about $28,000—but in truth we didn't need all that much. I sold my car and scraped together $9,000, and John contributed another $9,000, and we sold a share of the company to a mutual friend for the final $10,000 to put us in business.

Not incidentally, the *lifestyle* I was looking for checked in at around $100,000 a year. In my head, the lifestyle and the salary went hand in hand, and that was my target going into this venture. The round number would loom as the true measure of our success in our first year of operation; if John and I could each take out that kind of money, then surely we'd be a success. Now, we knew full well that a lot of people look to start their own businesses for all the wrong reasons. They think they can set out an arbitrary figure like $100,000, call it a starting salary, and count themselves successful. They think they can hang a sign on a door and all of a sudden the money will start pouring in. They think their time will be their own, and they can twiddle their thumbs on a boat or a golf course while their staff does the heavy lifting and keeps things churning. Sometimes they think that an idea alone is enough to set them apart or that the best way to avoid answering to a boss is to become one. Other than our hoped-for salaries, we tried not to fall into any of these traps. As a matter of fact, in my case, I tended to approach each decision from an oppositional perspective. As I've already indicated was my habit, I imagined every conceivable worst-case scenario and a few inconceivable ones as well, and if a prospect still looked good to me after I'd put it through that kind of wringer . . . well, then I'd give it some consideration.

I've always believed I absorbed this trait from my father, who was never a businessman himself but who tended to look at the world from a worst-case perspective. And yet, once he made a decision, he expected a positive outcome. That was his take on life, and it became my take on business: If you set out anticipating all kinds of setbacks and drawbacks and still find enough reasons to roll the dice and go for it, then you've prepared for every eventuality.

At Cigars Around the World, John and I had our contingencies covered. The worst-case scenario for us would be to blow our $28,000 investment, and that wasn't about to happen, primarily because there was no reason to dip into all of that money at the outset. We'd tap into it as needed and test the market each step of the way, to minimize our exposure. It wasn't seed money so much as gas money—a little something to put in our tank and fuel our early efforts and get us up and running.

John and I were doing our homework and covering all our bases, but we were flying mostly blind. John had a business school background—he earned his MBA the summer before we opened for business—but I didn't have any formal business schooling, so we developed our own hybrid style, mixing theory with practice. We didn't have a business plan, other than the obvious plan to take out more money than we put in. We had a strategy, an idea about how things might go, but I didn't know the first thing about spreadsheets and forecasts and projections, and I convinced John for the time being that those things wouldn't apply. One of the great buzz phrases in corporate America at the time was *practical execution*. In many offices, people spend too much time analyzing and scrutinizing every situation, and our mandate was simply to get on with it. Move forward. Make it happen. Run the ball into the end zone. It didn't matter how we did it as long as it got done, so we concentrated our initial efforts on drumming

Even small efforts loom large in a small business, and big efforts loom larger still.

up interest in our products and our membership packages. Everything else would have to flow from there.

We didn't have the money to buy a stash of cigars just yet, but we also didn't have any need to do so. The way we had the business set up, we'd work on a *just-in-time* inventory basis—that is, we'd take in what we'd need to fill each order. Not the best way to run a mail-order business over the long haul, but not a bad way to start. And besides, from our lowly cash position we didn't have much choice.

Our first order of business was to get the word out, and we looked to do it on the cheap. The rule of thumb in direct-response marketing, I quickly learned, was that you needed to make three impressions on a potential customer in order to make a sale; unfortunately we couldn't afford three impressions. Hell, we didn't think we could even afford a first impression, but we had to make some kind of noise. The best we could do was line up friends and family to hand out more than 100,000 flyers all over downtown Chicago, advertising our products and our membership concept—which as I've admitted wasn't all that unique except that we were now slotting cigars into a proven formula. At the same time, we began talking to cigar experts and importers to learn what we could about the business and to see about positioning ourselves as middlemen to an untapped customer base.

The leafleting effort was essentially a bust. Our so-called marketing staff consisted of our friends, siblings, cousins, and parents, and they all wanted to see us succeed, but we still had to keep them motivated. We sent them out onto the city streets as if they had a mission—and they did, for a time. In all, we spent a couple of weeks handing out those damn flyers in targeted neighborhoods, and the rate of return was abysmal. We worked in pairs and made a game out of it however we could—but of course we couldn't control the outcome. Once those flyers were stuffed into mailboxes or squeezed beneath windshield wipers, they were out of our hands. And we couldn't keep up the initial enthusiasm of our friends and family. We had them running all over town, and soon enough our "volunteers" started to ignore our phone messages when we called with a new assignment.

Unfortunately, the penetration on a low-end flyer campaign is almost always statistically insignificant. We knew as much going in, but we didn't exactly have a whole lot of options. Still, from the responses we were getting, we realized we would have been better off lighting those damn flyers on fire and sending our message across the Chicago skyline with smoke signals. In those two weeks, we maybe wrote thirty or forty orders tops, a percentage return that would run even the lowliest direct marketer straight out of business, and things weren't looking too promising.

It was November 1995, and we had positioned ourselves to capitalize on the traditional holiday selling season that runs from Thanksgiving to Christmas, but we had so far been relatively unable to tell the good people of Chicago that we were so positioned. It was the small-business version of the philosophical riddle about a tree falling in the forest with no one around to hear it fall: What if you started a business and no one knew about it? Really, we were nowhere, and every night when I went to bed I heard the needling of those metals guys, the unctuous charm of my old boss, predicting I'd be back begging for my old job. It was both a challenge and a warning. The familiar motivational line, which you can find in almost any business book, is that failure was not an option, but in reality I knew full well that failure was most certainly a possibility. We never choose failure, but sometimes it chooses us, and sometimes it finds us despite our best efforts. I worried we were on its short list of candidates for a humiliating defeat.

And so, in a desperate move, I put together a package of cigars and a covering note and walked it over to WLUP-FM, in the John Hancock building on Michigan Avenue, home of Jonathan Brandmeier's top-rated morning talk show. At the time he was Chicago's version of the irreverent morning drive-time deejay (he's since moved on to Los Angeles), and I thought what we were doing might strike some kind of chord with him and his listeners. I told him how I'd quit my job, how I was living with my parents, how I was betting everything on this little cigar business, how I had my parents and my sisters and my friends handing out these flyers.

It was such a long shot I didn't even bother to tell my partner John about it, because I knew he'd think I was wasting my time—because in all likelihood, I was.

Turned out Jonathan Brandmeier found something to like in my appeal. He had his producer call and invite us on his show, and that one appearance did the trick. It was a gold mine. Jonathan Brandmeier was funny, and he ripped into me mercilessly for still living with my parents. He also found some things to goof on John about, but he also sold the absolute shit out of our cigars. Really, he was amazing. We couldn't have scripted a better appearance, and he kept us on for half an hour, hamming it up the whole time. When we got back to the apartment our phones were going crazy.

I can't stress how important that appearance on Jonathan Brandmeier's show was to our successful launch, because without it we were toast; we would have likely stumbled through the Christmas selling season, hoping for a miracle, and then folded our tents and turned our sights to the next opportunity. We would have probably kept our start-up money, but we wouldn't have added all that much to the kitty. The flyers had produced just a trickle of business, nowhere near enough to sustain our hopes and dreams. It wasn't until this man put us on air and started thumping for us that we took off.

Was it just dumb luck, that this radio talk show host took a shine to what we were doing and broadcast it? Or was it the result of a successful promotional campaign? Okay, so maybe it wasn't a full-fledged *campaign,* but it was something. I sent out a whole bunch of packages—in boxes because a friend suggested that a boxed package is more likely to be opened by the intended recipient than a bubble-wrapped mailer or a simple letter. Each mailing, I'd try to do something creative, such as enclose a pair of glasses along with a covering note asking the producer to "take a closer look" at our exciting new gift ideas. Every day I'd pack and ship a few more, hoping someone would take the bait, so the old maxim that luck is the result of design holds at least partly true in this case. Clearly, if I hadn't reached out to Jonathan Brandmeier, he would never have stumbled across our little business on his own, but there's also the possibility that if he had passed on my pitch, there would have been someone else in the media to show some interest.

So who knows? The point is we kept taking our cuts in whatever ways we could afford, and once that initial appearance jump-started our efforts, we thought to dip into our as-needed reserves and support the promotion with a series of radio spots on the same station. Here again, this wasn't a business plan being carried out on a timetable. This was the two of us thinking a follow-up campaign a natural next move in order to build on and sustain the goodwill we'd been able to generate with the station and its listeners. That's what our seed money was for, after all, so we put it to good, specific use.

As soon as we got back to John's studio apartment after our appearance on the Brandmeier show, our few phones were ringing off the hook, and we began the real job of growing our business on the fly. We kicked into full-scale practical execution mode and mobilized our friends-and-family support team to man the phones and help with the shipping. We bought ourselves some time with our plan to send out a gift or acknowledgment card with each order, to be followed a month later by the first shipment of cigars, so there were a couple of weeks in there between our talk show appearance and the first few ads before we had to get our act together. We filled the time by making our first real hires, coordinating our packaging and shipping relationship with UPS, and expanding our base of contacts in the cigar industry. I even went out and researched what kind of fill we should use in our packages, settling on something called Kraft Spring-Fill, the same stuff they used in the Crate & Barrel shipping department. It was a little bit nicer than the garden-variety peanut-shaped fill, and it cost a little bit more, but we wanted to run a classy operation. For most customers, their first hands-on association with our product would come when they opened their first shipment.

To keep the ball rolling, we also sent out promotional packages to every like-minded radio station in the country. If there was an irreverent afternoon or morning talk show host on a Top 40 or Zoo-type station, we reached out to him or her

Grow your game to the next level.

with a box of cigars and a tailored pitch. And it paid off. I guess if it was good enough for the competition it was good enough for them, because talk show producers began calling to book us to talk about our cigars. If the numbers made sense we usually followed up these appearances with a series of advertising buys on each show that invited us on as guests, thinking that now that we had developed an audience we needed to reinforce the business.

Early on, we swallowed hard and bought our radio time with money we didn't have. It was a neat trick of courageous accounting and last-minute bill paying that we turned to our advantage. Most stations billed commercial time on credit, which meant that we could purchase, say, $20,000 worth of time on Z-100 in New York, and then hope like hell we'd get enough orders in the next thirty days to pay the bill. I tracked every ad as diligently as if I was using my own money to pay for it—which in fact I was. If a station wasn't delivering the same direct-response results as a competing station in the same market, I'd call and argue for a reduced rate or additional time. If I received no concessions, I'd pull the account. I'd check our call lists to see which times of the day were conducive to orders from our customers, and which were less likely to result in sales. And we staggered our ads in such a way that they didn't run during the same hour in several different markets because we simply weren't equipped to handle the call volume.

Naturally, we continued to look for "free" advertising opportunities wherever possible, selling ourselves as guests on talk radio stations or offering our cigars as premium items for station giveaways. These promotional mentions were invaluable, especially early on. At one point during our first six months in business, I tallied up how much free on-air publicity Cigars Around the World had received at stations all across the country and calculated that it was worth over $1 million in comparable commercial time. That's an incredible windfall for a direct-response business like ours, and a great boon to our bottom line.

In Chicago, we followed the Jonathan Brandmeier appearance with a turn on another popular radio show hosted by a shock jock named Mancow, and here again it lit up our phones. We gave away some memberships and had another good time, creating some additional buzz. From this point we made several call-in appearances on radio shows across the country—Los Angeles, Detroit, New York, Houston. If some producer wanted us, we were more than game. Judging by the bump in sales immediately following each appearance, the in-studio interviews worked best, but long distance we contented ourselves with a telephone interview on the theory that it was better than nothing.

We immediately started advertising on WLUP, and our new friend and champion supporter Jonathan Brandmeier embellished our spots and continued to blow some serious smoke in our direction. We even started advertising at other stations in the area and all over the country, earmarking a significant percentage of the money coming in for these media buys. One of our first significant ad buys was at WGN-AM, probably our biggest local station, with a reach all across the Midwest, and here we felt confident in our purchase because the father of my Elite Boat Wash and Wax partner was the chief financial officer of the Tribune Company, which owned the station, so at least I knew the ad salesman wouldn't be out to screw these two green kids with the mail-order cigar business.

In the thirty days immediately following our first

Brandmeier appearance, we took in over $150,000 in orders—all of it up front, so we were subsidized for the next while. It was still just the two of us, with a never-ending assist from friends and family, but at some point we recruited our buddy Kyle Koch to help us full-time, answering the phones and filling orders. As we raced through our first Christmas selling season it occurred to us that we might actually be onto something.

I was never the type to be easily satisfied, and once I'd seen the easy sales we could generate with a local radio appearance, I determined to make a bigger splash. Jonathan Brandmeier and Mancow had been great, and there was also a key assist from Spike O'Dell at WGN-AM, but an appearance on a national television show would push us off the charts. By this point I was getting good at these cigar-box promotional mailings, so I sent a whole bunch out to the network morning shows, such as *Today* and *Good Morning America,* and to some of the top national talk shows. The thinking here was to aim high, so I focused these efforts on national or syndicated programs.

Somehow one of these packages got into the hands of a producer for a syndicated talk show hosted by Danny Bonaduce, the former child star of *The Partridge Family* who'd gone on to build a career as a radio and television talk personality. His show happened to be taped in Chicago, and the producer wanted me to make an appearance. Only the segment the producer had in mind had nothing to do with cigars or our mail-order business. They were putting together an "eligible bachelors" show and had gotten it in their heads that I fit the bill.

As it happened, I was too busy ramping up this new business to have time for a relationship, so they caught me during one of my eligible periods, although I wasn't much interested in appearing on the show if I couldn't promote our cigars at the same time. But television producers are a feisty bunch when they set their minds to a thing, and these folks would not be put off, so I made them an offer. I asked if they were planning a holiday gift-giving show, figuring that most daytime talk shows likely devoted several segments to the holiday season. Sure enough, they were working on just such a show for the very next week, and I managed to barter my cigars onto the schedule in exchange for appearing on the bachelor segment.

It sounded like a good fit all around, and it might have been, except for the fact that the producers ambushed me when I showed up for the taping. Turned out they weren't shooting an "eligible bachelors" show after all, but an embarrassing segment they were calling "Dateless for the Holidays," which was pretty much self-explanatory and painted me as pretty pathetic. It didn't matter that the label fit, it was still plenty embarrassing, but I went through with it anyway and hoped no one I knew would be watching when it aired. (Yeah, like *that* was about to happen.) The producers held up their end of the bargain, though, and we sold a lot of cigars on the back of their holiday segment, so I counted it worth the humiliation.

Talk about taking one for the team, right?

The rush in business could not have come at a better time for our fledgling company. With each new appearance, there was another bump in orders, with the biggest bumps coming from those national television spots. We might have anticipated that the Thanksgiving-Christmas selling season would become our busiest period, but that first year it caught us somewhat unprepared. Our friend Kyle was working the phones. John's mother came out from Connecticut for a three-week stretch to lend a hand, and my father set aside his Ed.D. and went to work wrapping cigars in our stay-fresh packs and preparing them for shipping.

It was a real family operation, and we were all paddling the same boat. We might have lacked a little direction in those first frantic weeks, but we were all paddling.

One of the great charades in most start-up operations is playing up in size. At Cigars Around the World we were constantly creating the impression that we were bigger than we actually were, putting customers on hold while we

> **P**ay your key people as much as you can afford—and not as little as you can get away with.

checked a point of information with our nonexistent sales department or checking with some phantom shipping manager to see when a package had gone out. Commercial buys were negotiated by our so-called advertising department, and promotional giveaways were coordinated by our imaginary marketing team. In truth, it was often just John and me, and we wore so many different hats you'd have thought we had a giant staff.

Like it or not, all new businesses are judged by their size and scope, and here we couldn't boast all that much of either. Absolutely, we were just two guys working out of a studio apartment, but there was no need to advertise this fact when we could just as easily disguise it for the time being.

In our seat-of-the-pants way, with each significant new hire, we developed a fairly flat organizational chart. We looked at every member of the Cigars Around the World team as equally important, even during those first few weeks when we were staffed mostly by volunteers, a term I use only loosely because it's not like our friends and family had much choice in the matter. As we grew (and we grew quickly), there was no evidence of top-down management, and someone looking in on our efforts might have dubbed us a side-by-side operation. I became more of a coach than a boss, but I was a player-coach, for those of you who get the sports analogy. I was out there on the field, hustling along with everyone else on the team, but I also called the shots when we got back into the dugout. When we finally got into the habit of holding sales meetings every week, I'd solicit opinions across the board: Ben in shipping, Jennifer in sales, Brian in marketing . . . everyone was expected to contribute. (By this point, I should mention, there really *was* a Ben in shipping, a Jennifer in sales, and a Brian in marketing.) We'd all brainstorm on ways to have a better Father's Day, which in the cigar business is like a second shot at Christmas, or on different packing procedures to cut down on time and expenses.

We were all working toward the same goal. Here I borrowed a page from Ray Kroc, the founder of McDonald's, who made it a special point to keep his team happy. Legendarily so. This man created more millionaires on his payroll, through the distribution of stock options and special pension plans, than any other business leader of his time. He treated his people well, and I have to think they busted their butts for him in return. Regrettably, we were in no position to dole out stock options and special pension plans, but we could still treat our people well. I wanted our dedicated staff to have the kind of job security that the thirty-year metals salesman had been denied. Loyalty was all-important, and it was at the root of every business relationship we built and sustained. Our accountant, our lawyer, our shipping partners, the printer . . .

all the way down to the graphic artist we retained to design our logo and promotional materials. We told them all the same thing: Hey, you guys take care of us now, and we'll take care of you later.

We continued to work out of John's studio apartment for that first Christmas season, until finally we had to move. His landlord thought we were running a bookmaking operation, with the way the neighbors kept complaining about people coming and going at all hours. It was just as well, because we'd outgrown the place. We found a basement office in a nice professional building downtown and moved in just after the first of the year, and the great thing about this new space was that it was our own. We created a bright, fun environment for our expanding team—and a relaxed, laid-back atmosphere.

> Your management style should suit your personality. If you're shy and retiring, you'll never rally your team, so try another approach.

We looked on the stretch of time between New Year's and Father's Day as a point of pause, a chance to reflect on what had gone well during those first whirlwind months and where there was room for improvement. We also tried to look ahead and anticipate some of our needs going forward, and with this in mind I made a trip to Omaha, the call-center capital of the United States. Whenever you call an 800 number to make an airline reservation or to order flowers or to book a hotel, there's a good chance your call will be routed to an overflow call center, and there's a good chance that call center will be located in Omaha, where the flat Middle American accents of the locals come across like no accent at all. Of course I didn't know the first thing about outsourcing or overflow operations, but I learned quickly enough, and by the time I left Omaha I'd retained a top call-center company to handle all of the telephone orders that we couldn't manage ourselves. The way it worked was the calls would flow first to our bank of thirty or so phones in our Chicago office, and if those phones were busy or unmanned they would be routed to Omaha, where call-center operators would follow our set script and collect a fee for each call.

A word or two on outsourcing: it was a lifesaver. We couldn't afford full-time in-house professionals, so we farmed out certain tasks to experts in the field. And why not? John and I couldn't be expert in all aspects of our business, and besides, I'd rather know a little bit about a lot than a lot about a little. That's why this call-center service was key, and why we let UPS handle most of our packaging and shipping needs until we expanded into a warehouse with a mailroom operation of our own.

To man the phones in our office, we hired a bunch of college students and layered in all kinds of incentive opportunities and friendly competitions in an effort to boost sales. We brought in lunch for everyone and tried to make each day like a giant party. These young staffers worked for an hourly wage, but they also earned commissions and bonuses based on their sales. We really tried to make it an enjoyable place to work, and I think we succeeded, as evidenced by the fact that at the end of each day we couldn't get these people to leave. We'd crack open some beers and fire up some inventory and if the phones happened to ring we'd write up another order.

Over time, we discovered that our own people did a much better job converting callers into buyers and one-month memberships into multi-month memberships—by about a two-to-one margin—so we tried to service the calls in-house whenever possible. Still, a call center was essential backup. What this meant, though, was that we had to staff our phones from 5:00 A.M. until 10:00 P.M. Central Time, to handle the calls that would come in response to our morning and evening drive time radio advertising on either coast. It made for an incredibly long day, and for me and John there'd be no letup. One of us was on-site at all times, and during our busy seasons it was usually both of us, taking calls if that was what was needed or seeing to our endless shipping needs or working some new promotion.

Don't be afraid to delegate, but go it alone if you must.

We scored our first Father's Day push courtesy of *Good Morning America,* which selected Cigars Around the World as one of the top five gifts for the holiday, and the mention generated more than 3,000 calls in the first hour after our toll-free number was flashed on the screen. Three thousand calls! It was an incredible response, but we were prepared for it, and in many ways it signaled our arrival as an ongoing concern. We'd made it through our first big selling seasons and could look ahead with confidence to a bright future.

At the end of our first year we looked up and—lo and behold!—we had a business. A real, pulsing, thriving, growing business, spun from a lightbulb-over-the-head notion in a downtown café. It was a business unlike any other, except that our holiday seasons were brutal. Two weeks before Thanksgiving straight through to New Year's Day, there was no letup. That was the bulk of our year jammed into a seven-week period, and then we'd catch a breather for a month or two and come back for another killer few weeks just before Father's Day.

That first year, all told, we wrote just shy of $1 million in orders, generating about a 40 percent profit after accounting for rent, advertising, payroll, and cost of goods. And yet despite our runaway success, John and I didn't take out our $100,000 salaries that first year. We drew only enough to cover our needs, because we felt strongly that we needed to put that money back into the business. Yes, we'd written a mountain of orders, but we were also looking at a mountain of costs. Very quickly, we'd run our advertising budget up to about 25 percent of our cash flow—but we also realized we couldn't survive without it. The simple direct-response flyer campaign we'd attempted on our initial nothing budget had been wildly ineffective, while some of these spot commercial buys had a huge impact on sales. In just a few months, we outgrew our basement offices and had to expand our operations into a vacant warehouse out back—and it was a good thing too, because we would send out nearly 7,000 packages per month at the height of our business.

At one point very early on, we had a UPS on-line shipping unit installed, to help us handle the volume. Airborne, DHL, Federal Express . . . all the big shipping companies were pitching for our business. Even the U.S. Postal Service wanted in on our action, although we couldn't really consider them because at that time there was no way to track packages through the post office. UPS had been accommodating when we were just starting out and we remained true to our friends. Like I said, loyalty was all-important, and it walked a two-way street. (The UPS guy loved us, because his company paid him a piece-count bonus. He'd swing by our warehouse and pick up a couple thousand boxes and call it a very good day.)

One of the great lessons of this runaway start-up was passed on to me by a good friend of mine named Carson Sterling, whose family owned a lumberyard in downtown Chicago. He let me in on a family secret. He told me that one of the reasons their lumberyard had been so successful was that his family utilized every piece of wood, every scrap, every filing ... in order to maximize their returns. They even sold the sawdust and shavings that wound up on their shop floor, and when he shared this with me I started to think how to apply the same principle to the mail-order cigar business. The answer came soon enough. With our early success came a rash of inquiries from cigar manufacturers and marketers of cigar accessories, wanting to get in on our game. Their knee-jerk request was always to buy or rent our customer list, but I knew enough even early on to recognize this as our single greatest asset, so I wasn't selling. I wouldn't sell our client list, not at any price. Even if I had managed to negotiate a sweet deal to share the list with an outside company it would have been a shortsighted move.

Still, I wasn't above selling ad space in our packing boxes, and before that first year was out we were printing advertising inserts for lighters, humidors, cutters, carrying cases, hygrometers. Whatever these people were peddling, we'd let them reach out directly to our customers at a rate of $1 per box. Let me tell you, this became a tremendous source of found revenue for our company—and our way of selling the sawdust.

The bonus was that after some cigar manufacturers noticed the success these other accessory companies were having with ad inserts, they wanted a piece of the same action, so we started negotiating for Macanudos or Cohibas or Almirantes or some other premium brand the distributor wanted to get out to customers as samples. We'd get the cigars for free or at a greatly reduced rate and include them in our monthly pack, which slashed our cost of goods in some cases by 100 percent, offering manufacturers a great way to get customers to sample their cigars and hopefully turn into buyers by the box.

Everything's negotiable.

Another important lesson: Don't be afraid to ask for help. Friends, advisers, customers, employees, even competitors are often uniquely positioned to offer a meaningful assist, and as often as not they'll come through for you in important ways. This was reinforced for me after working so closely with Donald Trump, who's always asking his advisers, "What do you think of this?" He'll stop someone on the street to solicit an opinion on one of his buildings or one of his businesses, and he takes that opinion to heart. He makes his own decisions, mind you, and he takes responsibility for his own decisions, but they're informed by input from all kinds of people. In fact I had an opportunity to put this approach into practice when we were just starting out.

We had ramped up in no time at all, and as we looked ahead, we realized our strength was in our foundation. We had a growing customer base, but we weren't dependent on one single customer. We'd nurtured quite a few corporate accounts that first year, and we'd add many more in the years to come, but these represented only a fraction of our business. Our core customers were individuals, buying memberships for one-, three-, or six-month intervals, which meant that if we lost any single customer or group of customers we'd be able to take the hit. When you're just starting out, no order is too small. It didn't matter to me if someone wanted one stick or one thousand boxes, I'd sell it to them; we had a whole lot of chances to put this philosophy into practice. We weren't a cigar store, obviously, but every now and then someone would see our sign and wander into our office looking to buy a single cigar. And guess what? We'd sell it to that person, because that's how you make it in the cigar business, one cigar at a time.

Lessons Learned
ON LEADERSHIP

PLAN AT LEAST A COUPLE OF MOVES AHEAD Even our impossible dreams have a morning after. We live in a "What have you done for me lately?" world, and you'll do well to remind yourself of this each time you complete an assignment. When I started my first business, I didn't simply think in terms of growing that one business into viability. Not at all. It was about executing a simple concept, and then executing it better, and then building the result into an enterprise that could sustain us for the next while. Each success raised the bar on the successes to follow. At twenty-four, I wanted to start a business that would earn me a yearly salary of $100,000. That was my stated goal. But once I reached that target, I had another in my sights. Some weeks, there wasn't enough money to make payroll or pay off our vendors, but I was already thinking of generational wealth and acquisition targets and new business initiatives. Before I finished converting my first distressed property into luxury condominiums, I was casting about for a second property to develop. Why? Well, the successful entrepreneur can never be truly satisfied if he gets where he's going. Because let's face it, once you've arrived, you're done.

READ This one's a no-brainer, but you'd be surprised at how many successful people check their outside interests at the door once they put their name and title on it.

Keep your worldview as wide as possible. If you're in the widget business, it's not enough to know widgets. Celebrate your well-roundedness. Stay on top of public events and economic developments. Read at least two daily newspapers all the way through. Always have a book going. Learn a little bit about an awful lot and an awful lot about precious little. Consult your appropriate trade journals. Grow through the books and publications you read, the people you engage, the challenges you meet and master.

KNOW WHAT YOU'RE WORTH Put a price tag on your time. Really. Most of us at one time or another have started a sentence with the phrase "I wouldn't cross the street for less than . . ." It's a throwaway line, but it's worth noting here for the way it signals our impulse to measure our efforts. Does a $200-an-hour attorney volunteering at a local soup kitchen give more of his time than the minimum wage college student working the same chow line? Not exactly, but it's useful to weigh what we might earn in our professional lives against what we give up in our personal lives. It comes down to knowing who you are and what's important to you. Settle for less only as an investment in your future.

CONQUER THE FEAR FACTOR Might as well get in a subtle plug for another NBC reality show. Behavioral scientists suggest we are born with only two fears, the fear of falling and the fear of loud noises. The rest of our fears are learned, and if we learn to harness those fears and rise above them, they will melt away. (Anyway, that's the idea.) Challenge yourself and your team to overcome their greatest fears first and the lesser fears will seem smaller still. To put it in *Fear Factor* terms, if you're faced with a choice of eating a plate of snails, frogs, or chicken livers, and the snails freak you out the most, go for the escargot. And start with the ugliest, most disgusting snail on the plate. After that, everything goes down a little easier.

ANTICIPATE CHANGE About the only certainty in corporate America is that things change. Count on it. Every ten years, 65 percent of the companies in the Fortune 500 turn over. And it doesn't end there. Even the very nature of work and our all-important employee-employer relationships are in constant flux. In 1900, 50 percent of all Americans were self-employed. Seventy-five years later, that number had shrunk to just 7 percent, as corporate job security became the norm. But that all changed once again with the invention of the microchip, and the pendulum has swung back toward independence. Indeed, the more things change, the more they remain the same, and suddenly everything old is new again. Yesterday's bureaucracies are becoming more innovative and less traditional, while the job security of our parents' and grandparents' generations have become the career insecurity of today. All of a sudden, any job that is predictable is a job waiting to be cut. Creativity and adaptability are the only safe havens in the shifting seas of corporate uncertainty. Encourage these traits from your team; demand them from yourself; solicit them in the marketplace. And look ahead to the next big thing.

RELOAD Studies show that the average American will change jobs six to eight times during his or her working lifetime, and most Americans will change careers a couple times as well. That's a compelling reminder never to rest on your past accomplishments. The winning entrepreneur is never bored. If you've run through all the goals and challenges in one arena, look to another. Ronald Reagan managed two successful careers—as an actor and union leader—before embarking on a career in politics. Steve Jobs helped to ignite the personal computer revolution as cofounder of Apple Computers in 1976 before jump-starting Pixar, the award-winning studio that has produced some of the highest grossing animated films in motion picture history. Shake things up before you have a chance to grow restless. Aim high, and higher still.

PURSUE YOUR PASSION Okay, so maybe my partner John and I weren't exactly *passionate* about the cigar business, but it seemed like a lot more fun than selling widgets or tire irons. Get behind a product or an idea that you can see, feel, and taste (and in this case, inhale), and you'll stand a better chance of success.

GENERATE ELECTRICITY Hey, if it worked for Jack Welch at GE, it'll work for you. Even an armchair scientist will tell you that all electric current flows from voltage and amperage. Okay, great, but what does that mean to a would-be entrepreneur? Well, in a business setting, we can look on voltage as the potential in a new idea, team, or strategy, while amperage can refer to the energy we bring to that new idea, team, or strategy. You can't have one without the other if you mean to light things up.

GET OUT OF THE WAY The best leaders provide direction, support, encouragement, and incentive, but then they leave it to their team to do the job they were hired to do. Monitor progress and keep your hand in if you must, but let your people strut their stuff. It will give them more confidence and endear them to the cause, and they'll return the gift with hard work and dedication.

KNOW THE SITUATION I'm a big proponent of situational leadership. I don't know if that's what they call it in business school, but that's the label I've used to describe the flexibility all leaders must demonstrate in order to adapt to different challenges and personnel. Not every member of your team will respond in the same way to the same push, and not every push will result in sales. Note too that what works on one day with one group or task might not work on another day with the same group or task. Be firm and consistent, but go with the flow.

TRACK YOUR PROGRESS The best thing about a to-do list is seeing each item scratched off at the end of the day. The same holds for the targets we set for our business, for our team, for ourselves. The best managers *manage*—and they chart their progress in a systematic way. Evaluate your efforts on a regular basis and you'll be better able to assess what you're doing right, what you're doing wrong, and what you'll need to fix in order to get where you're going.

HIRE THE RACEHORSE Hit a mule and it just stands there looking at you. Hit a racehorse and it takes off. No questions asked, no reasons needed, no direction but dead ahead. Surround yourself with racehorses and you'll jump out in front; harness their energy and enthusiasm and you'll stay there.

ENCOURAGE STRENGTH BY EXHIBITING STRENGTH
Do this on the theory that tough times don't last but tough people do. Also, only the strong survive. And on and on. Search your *Bartlett's* and you will find a thousand quotes to illustrate the timeless link between strength and leadership. Check this one out: "O, 'tis excellent to have a giant's strength, but it is tyrannous to use it like a giant." True strength comes from wisdom and confidence, not from sheer power, and from that wisdom and confidence comes the power to quote Shakespeare as if you read it all the time.

LISTEN To your staff. To your customers. To your competitors. To your investors. To your industry analysts, even. Keep both ears to the ground in order to keep your other body parts aligned to the task. We wouldn't plow ahead toward our goal without first looking where we were going, so why solicit opinion or analysis with anything less than an open mind or an open set of ears? Sometimes when a particular approach is not working, a team leader is the last to know—and that usually happens when he turns a deaf ear to whatever it is he doesn't want to hear.

LEARN TO FISH WITH THE OTHER GUY'S BAIT Take every opportunity that comes your way, even if it's one you hadn't counted on or created. David Neeleman, founder and chief executive of JetBlue, the low-cost airline that has quickly earned a reputation as one of the most forward-thinking companies in America, makes it a point to work the line with his in-flight crews at least once a week. He gets pillows for passengers, pours drinks, and encourages flight attendants to bend his ear. He also makes it a point to fly the competition—coach. In this way, he has kept in constant touch with his market, his employees, his customers, and his product. And he has grown his company from a single plane operating out of JFK in 2000 into an industry force that dominates the New York–Florida markets and has recently opened up low-cost routes to California. Go the extra mile and discover new prospects.

THERE'S NO PLACE LIKE HOME Don't be afraid to set your sights on some far-off goal in some far-off place, but at the same time feel proud to pursue opportunities in your own backyard.

FIVE
Business as Unusual

The God of this century is wealth.

—Oscar Wilde

F ile this one under Do as I Say and Not as I Do: every sound business should begin with a business plan. I don't care if it's a hastily scrawled to-do list on the back of a barroom napkin or a thoroughgoing analysis complete with spreadsheets and assumptions, you need some kind of road map if you mean to make a go of any new venture.

That said, a business plan might have hurt Cigars Around the World. I don't mean to overstate the case, and I certainly don't mean to contradict myself—but hey, life is all about contradictions, and business is all about turning those contradictions into challenges. And let's face it, if there weren't exceptions to our rules of thumb, we'd be all thumbs.

I'll explain. We got our cigar business going on serious pluck and gumption, but I didn't know anything about business plans and my partner was content to proceed on my terms, despite his MBA. We had a simple idea and went with it. Each decision led logically to the next, and each decision made sense, but we never thought we needed to put something down on paper, to think things through to where we could make some projections. We must have thought business plans were for everyone else; we'd get by on bright ideas alone. We had one investor—a currency trader named Marcus Zwissig, a friend of a friend, at $10,000—and he didn't think to ask for a business plan, so we pretty much made things up as we went along, trying out different approaches until we found what worked.

Despite our hoped-for $100,000 salaries and our promising early sales, we didn't take out a whole lot of money that first year. In that one respect, that first year was tough. We felt it was essential to plow all our profits back into the business in order to grow our operation, and it was as well. I was still living at home with my parents, and John had his studio apartment, which had doubled as our base of operations for the first few months; we were too busy to have any expense worries. Anyway, we spent most of our time at work and took most of our meals there, so we figured we could do without a salary for the time being.

The Cigars Around the World staff, though, wasn't exactly willing to work under the same terms. Our first hire held out for a new suit as his entire compensation package, which I agreed to buy for him to use on interviews for a "real" job, but here again, that was the exception. Most people wanted to be paid a living wage, and in order to meet those unanticipated demands the management team—namely, me and John—had to forgo our own living wages for the first while. I'm reminded here of the philosophy of Ben Cohen and Jerry Greenfield—the founders of Ben & Jerry's, the Vermont-based ice cream company—who pledged to keep their salaries and those of their top executives at a relatively modest level above the salaries earned by their average full-time employees. Granted, it's a tough pill for some executives to swallow, but it's a great way to boost the morale of your entire company and to increase productivity and enthusiasm in the workplace. In our case it was a first-year necessity turned constant reminder that in success there is usually enough to go around.

As long as I have somehow journeyed to Vermont in this narrative, I'll mention an assist I received from John Sortino, the founder of the wildly successful Vermont Teddy Bear mail-order gift company, which in turn reinforces a meaningful point. I made a cold call to John Sortino as we were getting our efforts off the ground, wanting to pick his brain for advice, thinking he had traveled some of the same road during his start-up phase. Early on, I got in the good habit of reaching out to leaders in whatever industry I was pursuing, even to potential competitors, asking everything from ignorant to sophisticated questions about every aspect of their business. As long as they were willing to talk, I kept firing questions, and John Sortino had a great many insights to share. Like Cigars Around the World, his Vermont Teddy Bear operation began as a simple notion—that folks might be inclined to select and send a traditional gift sight unseen, with a telephone order—and he watched that notion grow into a multimillion-dollar business. Even his factory operation had become a popular tourist attraction after he added some family-friendly aspects.

I was surprised at how receptive this man was to my phone call, although in truth I shouldn't have been. As I've said elsewhere, it has long been my experience that most people genuinely mean well, and that given the opportunity, most would be only too happy to offer aid of some kind. Most people love to talk about themselves and their experiences.

John Sortino very graciously highlighted his advertising around second-tier holidays as a big boon to his early efforts. He would buy commercial time just before Valentine's Day or National Secretary's Day or Halloween, when ad rates were typically more affordable, and turn these occasions into gift-giving opportunities in the minds of his target audience. His great innovation, really, was to create holiday marketing opportunities all year long. I left our conversation vowing to borrow a page from his calendar.

By the end of our first year there was no denying the viability of our concept and the good living the entire Cigars Around the World family could draw from it. As we pressed forward we kept adding people and products and initiatives—and happily, customers as well. The mood of our staff was typically up, consistent with our sales. About the only downside to the business model we had all but stumbled across was that our traditional holiday season was always a killer. No matter how many people we had on our full-time payroll, it still meant six weeks of five in the morning to ten at night, from Thanksgiving to New Year's, which in Chicago coincided with the beginning and end of drive time radio on each coast. (In most markets, drive time programming tends to run from 6:00 to 10:00 A.M. in the mornings, and 4:00 to 8:00 P.M. in the early evenings, which in the Central Time Zone left us pretty much screwed.)

Borrow liberally to develop your own style.

Customer service was our hallmark. At $24.95, we offered an alternative to teddy bears or microbrewery beers in the area of impulse telephone-ordered gifts; and we encouraged customers to extend the gift for a period of months, all the way up to a full year—at which point, of course, we offered a thirteenth month free. The customer service kicked in with our 98 percent on-time fulfillment rate and our no-questions-asked return policy, and before long we started to notice repeat orders from the same customers year after year. As a matter of fact, we continue to service a few corporate accounts that have been with us since the very beginning.

If you charted our growth during this period you would have seen a steady line upward. Our annual sales topped out at just over $2 million in 1998, and there had been steady growth leading up to that point, beginning with first-year sales of around $1 million.

We tinkered with the formula as we went along, and had we been bound by a business plan we might have been inhibited from doing so. I was tipped to this possibility by my "adviser" at Vermont Teddy Bear, who cautioned that it's not always obvious who the gift givers are for a particular item. We started to realize from the market research we thought to do only *after* we were up and running that women tended to be the primary gift givers in a household, so we shifted some of our early print advertising efforts from publications such as *Esquire* and *GQ* to *People* and *Vogue*. Most of our advertising budget was devoted to radio time, but even in this area we shifted our focus from the irreverent morning shows that were most popular with male audiences to the Top 40 and Adult Contemporary formats that attracted more female listeners. After all, we had to be where we'd find the most potential buyers, right? And the shift seemed to be working, because we tracked each and every ad placement carefully and noticed an increasing number of women as repeat customers, giving our memberships as a kind of default gift to several men on their shopping lists.

But by 1999, things had taken an unexpected turn. Advertising rates at radio stations around the country skyrocketed—in large part, we surmised, because of the glut of venture capital money fueling the rise to prominence of all those dot-com companies. Much has been written about the great many high-tech start-ups that flared up at the turn of the last century, and the attendant speculation that helped spark a stock market frenzy, but there hasn't been much analysis of the ripple effect these high-flying companies had in the general marketplace. Their impact on the advertising industry was immediate and enormous, at least in our small corner. We were slow to realize that commercial time is sold according to supply and demand. We knew it, but then we set that knowledge aside because it didn't appear relevant. Consider: If a station can sell through its advertising time at full price, the ad salesmen are going to rethink their pricing and test the market at a higher level. The cost of doing business at the radio station remains the same, but the greater the number of advertisers wanting in on a radio station's commercial time, the better its bottom line.

All of a sudden, the cost of some of these radio spots started to get ahead of what we could comfortably afford, simply because there were more clients with more money looking to deliver their message to more people than ever before. Think back and you'll remember all these dot-com companies advertising like crazy during that period. A sixty-second spot on Z-100 in New York that might have cost us $800 the year before was now running $2,200—simply because that was what this new marketplace could bear. These suddenly flush dot-com advertisers didn't blink at these higher prices. They just gobbled up as much time as they could, blanketing the airwaves with their vague messages at whatever rate had been established.

This was all well and good for radio stations around the country, but it was doom and gloom for Cigars Around the World. We simply couldn't afford those rates; they would have bankrupted us. As it was, we were stretching ourselves with virtually every spot buy, counting on the direct response to bring in enough orders to offset the cost of the advertising time—and paying for those ads with the money collected from the resulting memberships. But the audience for these shows didn't double or triple to justify the bump in price; we weren't reaching any more listeners, and the ones we continued to reach weren't any more or less inclined to buy our cigars. Our model inched from practical to impractical with each successful dot-com launch, and I worried we'd be run out of business if we didn't come up with a new strategy.

Take nothing for granted.

The answer to our difficulties rested at the bottom of our bottom line. Up until this point, a segment of our operation we called on-premise sales had been accounting for about 10 percent of our revenues. We hadn't expected to do any business at all in this area, but once we were out there and making noise and positioning ourselves as high-end cigar retailers, we found a small but growing demand for point-of-purchase sales in nontraditional outlets. Cigar smokers could always go to a cigar store or tobacconist, but these outlets seemed to cater to the true cigar aficionado and almost always required a special trip. At that time, there were websites and catalogue companies that also catered to the sophisticated cigar smoker. And yet someone smoking a cigar for the first time or wanting to present a single fine cigar as a gift would often be at a loss wondering where to buy their cigars in a traditional bricks-and-mortar establishment, while others looking to celebrate a special occasion with an impulsive smoke would be at a similar loss. With this in mind, we began supplying our own humidors to restaurants, hotels, and country clubs, in an effort to boost sales. At the same time, we hoped, the reinforcement of the Cigars Around the World logo at the retail level would strengthen our brand.

It was a shift in strategy, to be sure, but we adopted it as a gradual process and a natural outgrowth of our core business. This approach goes back to our willingness to grow our company one cigar at a time, because there were some weeks when we went to service these new accounts when that was all we had sold—one cigar. It also goes back to the opening line of this chapter, about how most sound businesses begin and end with a business plan. In our case, the fact that we were operating by the seat of our pants allowed us to think outside the cigar box, and the fact that we were agile and unencumbered pushed us to try new things. The on-premise sales end of our business wouldn't even have appeared in an initial business plan, because it would never have occurred to us to seek sales in this area, but now that these sales had come looking for us, it made sense to go out looking for them.

With this dramatic bump in advertising rates, I started to pay some more attention to these afterthought sales, wondering if there was some way to increase their importance to our company as a whole. Certainly, with a little bit of attention and effort, we could step up that one segment and see what happened, so that's what I set out to do. One of the first moves I made in this regard really helped establish this new approach. I reached out to Ace Hardware and True Value, the country's two largest hardware store chains, and convinced their buyers to strike exclusive distribution deals with Cigars Around the World, allowing us to place our branded humidors at all of their checkout counters. The thought was that on a Saturday afternoon, when some home owner is out buying his lawn care products or home improvement kits, he'll catch a whiff of our fresh premium cigars at the checkout counter and impulsively buy one to enjoy that night after dinner. The idea was to create customers who more than likely wouldn't have thought to buy a cigar at all—let alone to buy it from some other source—and to grow those first-time customers into repeat customers.

It turned out to be a good move, even if it was born from desperation, and after just a couple months the True Value and Ace Hardware efforts began to pay off. These hardware stores are all independently owned; they're run as more of a retail collective than a franchise operation, and each store owner was free to make his or her own decision about carrying these humidors and positioning them. Still, we made a strong push at the trade shows and got enough of these independent store owners on board to make the effort worth our while, after which we expanded our reach into high-end steakhouses and hotel bars. Over time, casinos became a big part of this end of our business as well, eventually accounting for a huge chunk of our on-premise sales, and we established all-important relationships with casino managers all across the country.

This shift in emphasis to on-premise sales was all about

agility—and about being nimble and forward-thinking enough as a leader to champion such a shift on the fly. Had we been encumbered by a big-picture business plan, I might never have seen far enough down the road to recognize this all-important change in terrain, so a quick response to shifting market conditions was essential. One of the key moves I made during this transition period was to design a series of signature wooden humidors with a distinctive glass face featuring the Cigars Around the World logo, and to invest heavily in their manufacture. These soon became a fixture in restaurant bars and casino lounges and country club grill rooms. They came in all sizes, from a desktop number that held four boxes of twenty-five cigars all the way up to a giant cabinet that could hold as many as thirty boxes of cigars. My days were suddenly filled with sales calls, as I traveled the country nurturing relationships with restaurant, country club, and casino managers, hoping to convince them of the potential for profit in showcasing our cigars at their location.

See every angle.

None of this was anything like we'd expected going in or like our initial efforts when we were growing the company, but we were able to salvage a new business out of what was left of the old one. Here again, if we had been bound by a conventional business plan we probably wouldn't have been able to respond so quickly to the shift in the marketplace.

Eventually, the casino end of our on-premise sales effort started to do well. The beauty of the gaming industry, I slowly realized, is that they give stuff away; it's all about *comping* their best customers. A premium cigar is the perfect complimentary item to dole out to high rollers at the tables. At some of the bigger casinos—such as Harrah's in Joliet, Illinois, one of our earliest and most enthusiastic accounts—we'd have several locations on the floor, and the numbers couldn't help but add up. In a typical year, the casino would move about $100,000 worth of cigars, which meant that if we added a whole mess of casinos to our customer list, the result would be far more significant than found money to our company.

We even got into private labeling, which meant we could fashion custom cigar bands for country clubs and restaurants and special occasions. Once more this was an initiative that grew from without rather than from within. A client asked if we could brand a custom order for an additional charge. Frankly, the thought had never occurred to me. Once it had, however, I was all over it and set about highlighting this special service. I'd visit different factories in the Caribbean and order a special blend, which our people would then wrap with cigar bands featuring our clients' logo. Probably the biggest kick I got out of this end of our business was filling an order for Mike Ditka, the former coach of the Chicago Bears, who ordered thousands of Mike Ditka cigars to sell at his restaurants around Chicago—where he continues to sell them by the fistful.

In all, to borrow a couple of cigar-appropriate metaphors, we went from lighting it up to fairly choking, and back again to breathing in the sweet smoke of success with this shift in our focus. In the space of a year, we shifted from doing 90 percent of our business in direct-response memberships to doing 90 percent of our business in on-premise sales. In some respects, it's like we started a brand-new business within our existing business. Soon the *new* business eclipsed the old one, if not in initial sales, then at least in potential.

This was a complete turnaround, and there was a resulting shift in our workforce as well. Suddenly it no longer made sense to keep on all those hourly employees to answer the phones that no longer kept ringing. We didn't need all those hands in our shipping department to fill orders we no longer had. The call center in Omaha could handle any spike in our direct-response business, freeing our own people to concentrate on this new initiative. Naturally, our sales took something of an immediate hit, but since our payroll was down and our advertising costs frozen by the soaring rates, our expenses were also off, we were able to continue running the business at a nice profit.

> The more ground you cover, the more likely it is that you'll come across a good thing.

During this already tumultuous period, there were other changes I had to face. The first to surface was a growing split between me and my partner, John Cawley. As often happens in a partnership, he and I turned out to have different management styles and personal goals, and it's only natural that we weren't always on the same page. John was looking to expand his horizons and branch into the music industry, and I still saw opportunities in the cigar business, so we agreed amicably to part company. We'd had a good long run together and jump-started a profitable business, but our partnership had run its course.

Furthermore, I was approached by a Long Island–based holding company wanting to purchase Cigars Around the World, and this got me to thinking. I wasn't ready to sell, but I was ready to put a price on what we had built.

At around the same time, my father was diagnosed with kidney cancer, which set my entire family reeling and shook some sense into me regarding balance and priorities. I'd been a big proponent of maintaining some type of equilibrium between my personal and professional life, but I must admit that while we were getting Cigars Around the World off the ground, it was tough to shut off one valve for the sake of the other. I was all about work all the time, and I never really noticed or minded because I so enjoyed what I was doing. It didn't *seem* like work, so I never felt like I was missing out on anything. When my father got sick, though, I pretty much dropped everything to take turns with my sisters being with him in the hospital or keeping my mother company during those difficult, emotionally wrenching weeks and months. While I was going through this, I was reminded of the importance of family. There they were, our own personal lifelines, and nothing else seemed to matter.

My dad suffered for about eighteen months, and we all suffered right alongside him. He went through chemotherapy and radiation treatments and everything else his doctors threw at him, and with each disappointment he tried to keep cheerful and to keep fighting. Really, he fought like hell for the longest time, and at just about the end of his run it turned out he was eligible for a special stem cell transplant program being run out of the National Institutes of Health in Bethesda, Maryland, with Dr. Rick Childs. After a real hard sell from us Rancics, Dr. Childs took a chance and agreed to include my father in his program. Turned out my dad was the oldest patient on record to receive a stem cell transplant—by about twenty years!—and Dr. Childs took him on because he had been in such tremendous shape before he took ill. For that we'll all be eternally grateful.

My mom took an apartment in the D.C. area and waited out the treatment with my father. She was like a rock throughout the entire ordeal. She never left his side. I'd fly back and forth each week, to visit with my father and give my mother a much-needed break. For a long stretch of time I was spending three days a week in Chicago and four days a week in Bethesda, or four days in Chicago and three in Bethesda. It was tough to focus on any one thing. We all moved about like we were in a fog, unable to focus on any one thing but each other.

All of a sudden, the cigar business was the furthest thing from my mind, and it didn't matter if John Cawley bought me out and ran the company into the ground, or if I ran it into the ground myself. There would always be another business, another opportunity, but I had only one family and one father, so I set all these matters aside so that I could take care of business at home.

My approach to work was transformed by my father's illness. In traveling the country calling on new accounts, negotiating through my stalemate with John, and flying back to be at my father's side, I began to realize that some of the juice had gone from my days. Joy and excitement had been replaced by tedium and tension, so I vowed to shake things up once more. I even talked about this with my father, who had always been our greatest champion in whatever we kids set out to do. He was with me on the ground floor of the cigar business, helping to ship our first orders from our makeshift "mailroom" in my partner's studio apartment, but more than that, he spent his life helping us to set our bars high. And in my case, when I was just starting out, I think I did my reaching as much to please him as to satisfy myself.

In the end, sadly, my father lost his battle with cancer, and I lost my rudder for a stretch of time while I came to terms with his death. And I came to realize what I knew all along—that losing a parent sucks. It sucks in theory and in fact, and here it sucked most of all because it was *my* father. In honor of his memory I promised myself to set things right at work, to live my life going forward in such a way that it wouldn't be just about the mad scramble to make a living; it would be about the living itself.

When I focused on work again, I bought out my partner, redoubled my efforts in this on-premise sales push, and thought about resuming discussions with the company that had expressed an interest in buying us out some months earlier.

The sale of Cigars Around the World had its roots in our shift in selling strategy, because I first met our suitor, Mair Fabish, at a cigar convention in Las Vegas, where we got to talking. Mair thought our company might be a good fit with his Synergy Brands, a Long Island–based holding company with a concentration in business-to-consumer websites. Synergy was in an acquisition mode and liked our growth potential. At the time I couldn't really blame them—I liked our growth potential too, so I wasn't much interested in selling. Nevertheless, we kept in touch, and Mair looked on with interest as I reinvented our approach. He continued to see a tremendous upside in Internet sales, which to date had represented only a small portion of our business.

With John Cawley off pursuing his career in the music industry, Cigars Around the World was mine to grow. With the promise I made to myself at my father's death to embrace each new day at work as if it was the first instead of just one of many, I considered what a deal with Synergy might look like and how it might liberate me from what had become a constant sales effort. I've always maintained that it helps to set out the parameters of a situation, to see what it looks like from all sides. In this situation I wanted to have a clear understanding of what I might gain by selling and what I might keep by holding fast.

On the face of things, I didn't have much to complain about, regarding the Cigars Around the World gig. I had finally blown past that $100,000 salary target I'd set for myself when we were just starting out. I drove a nice car, paid for by the company. I ate out in nice restaurants, paid for by the company. I traveled the country and stayed in first-class hotels, paid for by the company. I wasn't making a fortune, but I had built up considerable equity in this business, as evidenced by Synergy's initial offer, and I could certainly have stayed with the program for several years more, but I was growing restless. I wanted to try something new. And I worried we would shoot right past the ideal time to sell, when our business still looked promising. About the last thing I wanted was for our fortunes to drift from promising to dubious before acting on Synergy's interest. I put in a call to Mair Fabish, to jump-start our conversation, realizing full well that in doing so I had cost myself some significant upper hand in whatever negotiation might follow.

> Sell from strength, absolutely. But even more important, sell from certainty.

What was Cigars Around the World worth now that our initial concept had morphed into a boutique cigar store operation? Well, it was tough to put a number on it, but I'll set out here what I wanted out of the deal, the same way I laid it out for the folks at Synergy. I wanted to stay involved, either as a consultant or a member of the board or both. I wanted my key people to have an opportunity to stay on as well, with long-term contracts and a sizable pay increase, to offer them the kind of job security I could never have afforded to give them on my own. And I wanted the Cigars Around the World name to live on, not to be swallowed up or otherwise put to rest with some other Synergy acquisition.

Reasonable requests all, and Mair Fabish and the Synergy board couldn't deny a single one of them, so that's pretty much how our deal shook out. I banked a nice chunk of change and continue to work for the company and serve on the Synergy board.

As of this writing, it remains a fruitful association all around. Synergy has done well with Cigars Around the World, my core sales and marketing people remain on board—including Jennifer Davenport and Ben and Rick Torres, who had been part of our team from the very beginning—and I continue to draw a nice salary and benefits package that provides a cushion for everything else I do.

The *everything else* has been interesting, and I'll get to it here. I realized in selling the cigar business that creating value was an important motivator for me, and along came an opportunity to create value on a different scale. Realize, after so many years pursuing a business opportunity where our success was measured—literally!—by how much of our inventory went up in smoke, it was a gratifying thing to be able to point at our brand and think, Hey, I built that. And so when the chance came to build another property—a run-down four-unit apartment building in Chicago's East Village—I grabbed at it.

Here's how that opportunity came about. A good friend of mine named Stuart Miller is a top real estate developer in the city. Our friendship had interesting roots. I used to date his sister-in-law, and when that relationship fizzled, I still

had this friendship with Stuart. We each had our own entrepreneurial take on the world and liked to bounce ideas off
each other to see if some new venture or notion made sense.
We used to sit down over lunch and talk about whatever was
on our desks or on our minds or in our datebooks. I was always fascinated by the ways he managed to create lasting
value from nothing at all, and the good money he managed to
make in the bargain.

At some point, we got in the habit of driving together to
our lunch dates, and I was impressed at the way Stuart was
able to drive through all these different neighborhoods and
point to this or that building and say, "Hey, I built that."
Clearly, he took the same pride in what he had built as I had
taken in building my business—except in Stuart's case the
results of his efforts were far more obvious. He created
value in terms of his own portfolio and real, tangible value
for his customers as well; he built their homes, and in so
doing he reached people where they lived.

Whatever else he happened to find on his bottom line, I
thought this was pretty cool.

Over a period of several months, our lunches became a
short course in property development. Stuart had it in his
head that I could pursue these same opportunities on my
own, and soon enough he had put the idea in my head too.
With my day-to-day involvement in the cigar business wind-
ing down, I was looking for some new outlet for my energies,
and as Stuart talked, I took notes. He was all excited about
this four-unit property, which of course got me all excited
about it—that is, until I actually eyeballed the place. It was
run-down, nothing special—nothing more, really, than the
shell of a building. Stuart looked at the place and saw opportunity, while I looked at it and saw only a mess. If I said any-

thing at all, it was probably along the lines of "You have *got* to be kidding."

But Stuart wasn't kidding. He knew what he was doing, and I could either trust him or move on. I didn't have the first clue about construction or property values, but I knew the East Village was an up-and-coming neighborhood, and that the key to doing deals at this end of the market was to buy on an upward trend. The details of the renovation would come to me soon enough, and I had every confidence I'd be a quick study. I had gotten up to speed in the metals business and had mastered the cigar business pretty quickly as well, so I figured construction would be a piece of cake, especially if I surrounded myself with good people I could trust.

> Trust your instincts.

The price tag on this fixer-upper was $365,000, and I decided to go for it. Paid pretty close to full price, as I recall. Stuart had some contracts in his car, and we generated the paperwork on the spot—probably to ensure that I didn't have a chance to talk myself out of it, but also because there were other buyers who had expressed interest. I guess Stuart didn't want the property to get away from me, and he didn't want me to get away from the property. He would have been interested in the property himself, but his company was mostly involved in fixing up apartment buildings and managing them as rental units. The numbers on this property made sense only if I sold the four units as quickly as possible, for as much money as possible.

It was a huge shift for me, but I had reached the point where I felt I needed to try something new, and I had a good and trusted mentor on board to help me through my paces. I thought, at \$365,000, plus the cost of the renovation, this property was a risk worth taking. Even if the market soured or I underestimated my building costs, I'd still own a sellable piece of property in an up-and-coming neighborhood. A conservative businessman always thinks of his money as being at risk when he makes an investment, but here that risk was capped by the market prices in that part of the city. I might not make as much money as I was hoping to make, but I didn't think I could lose all that much.

Basically, what I was buying was an empty lot with all the necessary zoning already in place. A patch of dirt with paperwork. The building itself—what there was of it, anyway—was just a bunch of bricks in the shape of building, with no real interior. The entire place would have to be gutted, but it was a happening neighborhood, close to the trains, centrally located, about two miles west of the Gold Coast area. All around, young professionals were flocking to the area, and it seemed a sure thing that I could find another four of them to flock to this particular building once I'd fitted it out with granite countertops, hardwood floors, picture windows, high-end fixtures and appliances, and all the other bells and whistles and luxury improvements such buyers had come to expect.

I'd just bought my first house, and I used the equity in my new home to finance the purchase and renovation of this East Village property. I wound up spending another \$310,000 fixing the place up. Stuart hooked me up with his general contractor, his electrician, his plumber. He turned me on to all of these great honest, hardworking tradespeople, and he made himself completely available each step of the way. He was a mentor wrapped inside a guru, masquerading as a personal trainer, and he walked me through the entire project.

Amazingly, we never once discussed the idea of throwing in together on it—I guess on the theory that I would have to fly solo at some point and I might as well earn my wings first time out.

From start to finish, my mentor/guru/personal trainer was completely available, reinforcing once more my theory that people genuinely want to help, especially if they have received a helping hand themselves. The most incredible aspect of his generosity was that it was so freely and joyfully given. Stuart never once asked for anything of me in return, other than I pay attention and give him the benefit of the doubt, which I was only too happy to do. He was just a good buddy, anxious to help another friend the same way he'd been helped when he was just starting out. He came by to check on my progress almost every day, and he was available to troubleshoot any situation that came up during the renovation. From time to time, he would even walk through the units with me and help me to figure out if we needed to move this wall, take out that closet, or open up that floor plan a little bit. He taught me to think like my own target buyer, so I tricked these units out with every last feature I'd want if I had been buying one of the things myself. I always had a thing for stainless steel appliances, so I put in stainless steel appliances. And off-street parking was invaluable in that part of town, so I had the place landscaped to accommodate a parking slip out back for each unit.

Improve on a proven strategy.

I sold the first three units in forty days, confirming our hunch regarding the neighborhood and validating the effort on this renovation. The fourth and final unit took another couple of weeks, primarily because it wasn't completed when I put the first three on the market. All told, after the brokerage commission and closing costs, I took in just over $1 million on all four units, leaving me with a sweet six-figure profit and an in-out turnaround time of less than thirteen months. I signed those contracts and thought, if this don't beat the tar *and* nicotine out of the cigar business, then I don't know the first thing about cigars or real estate. In my best year at Cigars Around the World, I'd never seen anything close to that kind of money—not in my own pocket, anyway—and here I'd worked this deal on the side, part-time, and flipped the thing for the kind of percentage gain that left me thinking it was all too easy.

Of course it *wasn't* easy, and development jobs don't always proceed so smoothly and deliver such a handsome rate of return, but it was something to think about—especially in a booming real estate market. Indeed, the building project left me thinking I'd been treading water in the cigar business for the past couple years, and wondering where I could find new challenges and new outlets for my creativity. As I did so I realized I need look no further than the project at hand. Even before I put those four condominium units on the market, I started looking for another property I could buy under something like the same terms.

I found one soon enough. Actually, I found two—one on the south side and the other on the west side. I looked at the west side property first, and here again it was a nothing building on an everything parcel. The value was in the land and in the permits and approvals that came along with it; the building would wind up costing me more money to tear down than it was worth. The seller was asking way too much money for it, but I put in a lowball offer and figured I'd never hear back from him. At that point, knee-deep in new bathroom fixtures on that first East Village property with my new house already leveraged to the max, I didn't think I could carry more than one additional renovation project until I had sold through the first, so I kept looking for a suitable investment within my limited means. I had the time to work more than two projects at once, but didn't think I could get my hands on enough capital to finance that kind of load, which was why I was all over the south side property when it surfaced on my radar.

Pursue every lead as if it's got your name on it.

This new property was another dump in virtually the same nice East Village neighborhood, about to happen in the same big way. It was actually a pretty unique setup, with three apartments in a building toward the front of the property and two additional townhouse units in the back, all located on a good-size corner lot on a street where there were a lot of properties in play.

Because of the zoning and the permits already in place, there were opportunities to add all kinds of value—shifting a wall, raising a ceiling, lowering a floor—and I walked the grounds with Stuart and imagined the possibilities. I was able to purchase the building for just under $500,000, which I considered a bargain with the renovations I had in mind and the value I'd be able to add to the property. The projected costs of renovation checked in at just under $500,000, which if we came in under budget would put me into it for about $960,000—more money than I had ever put on the line for any one deal, and enough to keep me up nights if I hadn't had a strong feeling that there was a rich opportunity here.

Understand, I still had my four condominium units from that first building when I closed on this second deal, so virtually all of my money was tied up in these two properties when that overpriced west side property resurfaced as a prospect. The owner called me up and asked me if I was still interested. I no longer had the resources or the line of credit I had had at the time I'd made my lowball offer, but I told him yes, of course I was still interested, provided he would come down to meet my offer. It was such a sweetheart deal: The value of the land itself was actually greater than $425,000, what I'd offered, and yet the property featured two workable building footprints and all the zoning and permits we'd need to get going.

Trouble was, I couldn't swing it on my own. Even at this lowball level, I was already stretched too far to get a conventional loan from a bank, and I couldn't even dig deep enough to cover the down payment on an unconventional loan. I reached out to another real estate developer I knew in the area, someone who had always said that if I was looking to partner on a deal I should give him a call. His name was Jim Malecky, and he ended up kicking in $160,000, which represented 20 percent of my projected total costs and therefore just enough to secure a loan, so I counted him a 50 percent partner in return. And I counted myself lucky that he was interested in the deal at all. He had what I needed, so I had to cut the pie down the middle—but that's how it goes sometimes, when you're spread so thin.

The real estate business, I quickly learned, was not without its occasional surprises. Everything had gone so well on that first renovation that I was unprepared for the snafus in these subsequent efforts. I had to fire a contractor after he all but fell asleep on the job. A crazy neighbor pulled a gun on me. Estimates turned out to be little more than uneducated guesses. Glitches with the city's building department shut me down or otherwise set me back. There were daily headaches that taken together could have added up to a migraine. I used to call Stuart to get his help navigating these various troubles, and he would always marvel at my run of bad luck. No crazy neighbor had ever pulled a gun on him, he said. No contractor had ever fallen asleep on his job site. He had me thinking I was snakebit—but the truth was none of these problems were so big that they couldn't be gotten past. They were hassles, nothing more.

That is, until the fire. A big, television-newsworthy fire—and it just about knocked me on my ass and put me out of business. (Of course, Stuart never had a fire like this in one of his buildings, he was quick to mention, even as he was quick to help me through it.) It was the Thursday night before the Memorial Day holiday weekend. Renovation on the west side property was going great guns. We had framed everything out. The rough plumbing was in. Heating, ventilation, and air conditioning (HVAC) were in. The guts were all in place, about 60 percent of our construction dollars were already spent, and we were looking at mostly cosmetic and finishing work from here on in. Countertops, fixtures, windows, landscaping . . . that was all still to come, but we were nearly there.

I was out at a bar, sidling up to some girl, longneck beer in hand, when my cell phone rang.

The guy on the other end introduced himself as Chuck from the Busy Bee board-up company.

"Your building's on fire," he said matter-of-factly, like he was calling to tell me my suit was ready at the dry cleaner's. "Do you want us to board it up for you when the fire's out?" he asked.

I figured it was some kind of prank call, so I hit the End button on my phone and went back to my conversation with this girl. I was a successful young businessman out for a night on the town, and I couldn't be bothered with such nuisance calls. These board-up guys were like the ambulance-chasing lawyers of the urban real estate business.

A couple of minutes later, the phone rang again. Another board-up company and another appeal for my business. By now I was thinking something wasn't right. One call might be a prank or a mistake, but a second call might make them both legit. These board-up guys have got people listening in on police and fire department scanners, hoping to be the first to respond to a fire so they can win the contract to board up the burned-out building.

The phone rang three or four times more in just the next three or four minutes, but after the second call I excused myself from the lovely lady I was pursuing, hopped into a cab, and made my way to the property. (Even Chicago's most eligible bachelors have responsibilities.)

"I think one of my buildings might be on fire," I said. For all I knew it came out sounding like a line.

I headed toward the west side property expecting the worst, and as I approached the street and started to see all these red lights flashing, my heart sank. I went from thinking *No way is this building on fire* to *Oh, shit, it's on fire* in the space of a city block. The street was blocked off. The power was down. At the scene were a hook and ladder truck, news camera crews, and more uniformed officials than I cared to count. As I muscled my way past the police barricades I had a sick feeling in my stomach. I tried to keep calm, because I knew there was nothing I could do at that moment but wait for the blaze to die down.

It was only money, I told myself, but the sick feeling had to do with the fact that it was someone else's money. It was devastating to see my efforts ablaze in the night sky, but the most disturbing element was that it was someone else's money on the line along with mine. Remember, I had a partner on this deal, and I wasn't about to let this guy lose his money. I'd take the hit if I had to, I told myself, but he would come out whole. Even if I had to sell my own house to make good on his investment, that's what I would do, and I remember thinking of my father at just that moment. Flames were dancing in and out of our framed-out windows. There was smoke and commotion and charred debris underfoot—a sad, depressing, disturbing scene. All I could think of was doing the right thing by my partner on this deal, because my father had always taught me that my good name (which of course was his good name too) and my reputation were my greatest assets.

So as I stood there on the street, watching one of my most significant single investments go up in smoke like one of the cigars I still sold for my safety-net living, I realized that all good deals come down to my name and my reputation. The fallout from this fire was a mess; for a while my name and my reputation were pretty much shot. The project had been nearly complete, and I had already spent the bulk of my renovation budget, but the claims adjusters evaluated the property as if

> When things don't go your way, never forget who you are, and always remember the bigger picture.

it was still the run-down building I'd purchased some months earlier. Plus, there was an ongoing arson investigation; fire department officials tried to determine the source of the fire and insurance adjusters waited for the results of that investigation. No one ever came right out and accused me of arson, but clearly somebody suspected me or one of my people—which I suppose made sense considering how much money was involved. Initially, it seemed unlikely I'd ever get all of my money back, and that I would indeed have to find some way to come up with $160,000 for my partner Jim Malecky. I had no intention of tying up his money in a protracted battle with the insurance company—not after he had placed his trust in me and helped me to get this project off the ground.

Actually, Jim couldn't have been nicer about it when I called him with the initial bad news, and with each update he was more and more understanding. "Hey," he kept saying, "let's just see what happens." He considered himself a full partner in the deal, same as me, and if I was prepared to take a hit with the insurers, then he felt honor-bound to take the same hit as well.

In the end, I had to hire a claims adjuster to negotiate a settlement with the insurance company, and the adjuster was aided in this effort when local police were finally able to pin the fire on a group of neighborhood kids who had been out to amuse themselves at the expense of the yuppie developer who was looking to gentrify their street. The insurance company still wouldn't look beyond the property's original evaluation, but at least the source of the fire was cleared up. In my head, I went from thinking I'd score another nice windfall on this project when things were going well, to thinking I'd be wiped out by the damage, to hoping I'd at least get our money out after the settlement, to finally realizing I'd take a hit of $50,000 to $100,000, depending on my final costs and the ultimate selling price of the units.

It was bad, but I contented myself with the knowledge that it could have been worse. I reminded myself that most businesses encounter these types of setbacks all the time. The bigger the venture, the bigger the setback. I'd been disappointed before—when the ink ran on all those boats up in New Buffalo; when our initial leafleting campaign at Cigars Around the World proved a complete bust—but those had been small disappointments compared with this. I rallied behind the notion that someday, when my ventures had grown bigger still, even this fire will loom as a small disappointment by comparison.

Indeed, when the smoke finally cleared on this project, and the claims adjusters managed to squeeze about fifty cents on the dollar from our insurance company, I would put my name and my reputation on the line once more—this time, in the biggest challenge of my adult life. It would be unlike anything I'd ever done before.

Lessons Learned
ON VISION

BUILD A LIKE-MINDED TEAM Surround yourself with smart, hardworking, self-motivated people who share a common goal. If they happen to be people you wouldn't mind having a beer with, then so much the better. If they happen to be smarter, harder-working, and more self-motivated than you, then so much the better on these fronts as well. Let it elevate your game before you let it get you down. I don't know about you, but I find that I thrive in a team environment, feeding off my colleagues in such a way that we make each other better, faster, stronger, smarter.

ACCEPT BLAME If you miss the mark, you miss the mark, but no leader ever hit his target the next time out by pointing fingers. Accountability is crucial, and heads must sometimes roll when a project or initiative fails miserably. (Think George Steinbrenner and the dozen or so batting coaches he has fired over the years when his team has failed to hit.) But the ultimate responsibility always rests upstairs. Take it, learn from it, and move on.

INSPIRE Why does man march willingly into war? Well, we live in a complicated world where some answers are no longer clear-cut, but it used to be that a soldier fought for his ideals and for the guy in the foxhole alongside him. Bring about that kind of dedication in your troops and you'll move them successfully into any battle.

SET THE STANDARD Team members look to their leader for more than just leadership, and if we mean to succeed, we'll need to model all kinds of positive behaviors. Remember, the standards we set for ourselves become the standards we expect from others.

MAINTAIN AUTHORITY BY DELEGATING AUTHORITY Our best leaders have the ability to hand off an assignment to just the right person at just the right moment. These same leaders also recognize that there are times when if they want a job done right, they have to do it themselves. Discover the best in yourself and the best in your team and put the whole package to work.

PUT YOUR MONEY WHERE YOUR MOUTH IS A lean operating budget will keep a company in fighting trim if the bosses' salaries are in line with everyone else's. Tighten your own belt before asking your employees to tighten theirs.

DEVELOP A CONTRARIAN VIEW Folks who gamble on sporting events have a theory: Bet away from the nation. If you take comfort in the fact that you think like most people, then you probably *are* like most people. To change your life, you might need to ignore your instincts and swim against the stream. Realize that by the time you reach the age of sixty-five, most of the people you went to high school with will be either dead or dead broke. If your goal is to be among the rest, you need to start thinking for yourself. Bet away from the nation.

REJECT CONVENTIONAL WISDOM Or, at least, consider the source. Most tried-and-true methods of doing business were at one time or another considered radical. In order to survive and thrive in today's marketplace you'll need to develop a few radical approaches of your own. It's up to you to invent your own rules as you go along. I'm not suggesting here that you refuse to play by everyone else's rules, but to do so at the expense of any other approach is to risk complacency. Look around: There is almost always a better way.

DO NOT TURN ONE BLUNDER INTO ANOTHER Mistakes can be contagious, and the best way to stop the spread of mistakes is to figure out what went wrong. The forceful leader knows how to reconnoiter, reshuffle, and regroup. The winning team player knows how to make the adjustment.

MINIMIZE THE DRAMA IN YOUR LIFE Your level of success will be determined by your ability to focus, which in turn will be shaped by the focus of those around you. Avoid the drama kings and queens who are constantly calling attention to themselves and away from the tasks at hand. Keep your professional and personal relationships positive and productive, avoid those that prove petty and problematic, and you will move forward. And remember, small minds discuss people; average minds discuss events; great minds discuss ideas. Only you can set the agenda for the discussions of your life.

LOOK BACK TO LOOK AHEAD There's no use fretting over spilled milk, even though there might be everything to learn from the spilling. When things go wrong in business, they tend to go wrong for a reason, and success comes to those who set things right. Most businesses can survive a couple of hits. Make every effort at damage control before you take a knockout blow.

DO WHAT YOU CAN I've never been one for that reach-should-exceed-your-grasp stuff. Better to have a B idea and to execute the hell out of it than to spend all of your time polishing an A idea that gets you nowhere. Grab whatever you can reach and reach where you must, but know that it's the doable ideas that get carried out.

OWN INITIATIVE Be the driving force behind your company's new ideas. Find room in your thinking for the innovations and approaches that under different circumstances might never have occurred to you.

SEAL THE DEAL Handshakes are fine. Contracts are better. And both should be revisited on a regular basis.

COUNT ON FAMILY I would have never gotten Cigars Around the World off the ground if it weren't for the efforts of my parents and sisters (and aunts and uncles and cousins). That's the great thing about family members. They'll work cheap, even discounting for the emotional toll that sometimes comes as a result. Abuse their generosity and let them abuse yours in return, and relish in the abuse you give each other. The other great thing, for most of us, is you can trust family members. Rely on their counsel and support. Model your days on your mother's and father's. Pick your uncle's brain. Learn from their experience. Blood *is* thicker than water. Of course, the flip side to this is that it also stains, so we should celebrate the marks left on us by our families before we run from them.

TAKE EVEN THE WORST OF THINGS IN STRIDE It's okay to let a personal tragedy derail you from your plans. Indeed, it's often necessary. But get back on track before you no longer remember where you were heading.

DO YOUR THINKING AND ANALYSIS AWAY FROM THE OFFICE There are only so many hours in the day, and if you're heading up the efforts in your workplace, you'll need to spend that precious time on the pressing business at hand. Nights and weekends (or early mornings if you're up before the sun), you can devote to planning and other big-picture issues, but when that clock is ticking you should focus on the comings and goings and doings and not-doings of your entire operation. There are enormous benefits to keeping your head in the clouds, but do it on your own time.

SEE TO IT THAT THINGS END WELL You never know when you might cross paths with a former associate, a rival, an old friend. Part on good terms whenever possible. Your girlfriend's brother-in-law just might turn out to be a lifelong friend and business mentor.

THINK LIKE A BIG FISH IN A SMALL POND The chance to make a splash is often too good to pass up, and with this in mind small markets can sometimes offer the perfect locus for your big ideas. I'm reminded here of the decisions facing former President Bill Clinton when he graduated from Yale Law School. Like the rest of his class, Clinton was wined and dined by some of the oldest, most prestigious law firms in New York. Generally speaking, he could have written his own ticket at any top firm anywhere in the country. But Clinton turned his back on the big-city, high-salaried offers that came his way and looked instead to his home state of Arkansas. In so doing, he paved the way for his own personal success story, becoming governor at thirty-one and using that office as a springboard to the White House. The parallels to our own endeavors are everywhere apparent. You don't have to be the biggest to be the best. Become a dominant player in a niche market, and grow your efforts from there.

MAINTAIN FOCUS In my discussion of the changing face of our cigar business, I write with some foolish pride that we launched our efforts without a traditional business plan, but that was just dumb luck that happened to play in our favor. Virtually every successful business needs a road map, and virtually every road map takes into account the twists and turns you'll likely find along the way. Without a plan of some kind, you'll lack direction and focus. Lay out a plan. Keep it simple. Systemize your approach. Develop a to-do list and a not-to-do list. Be efficient and effective. Keep your eyes on the prize—and don't be afraid to change the prize if you shoot past your incentives.

STRIVE My all-time favorite fortune cookie: "A gem cannot be polished without friction, nor man perfected without trial." True success means constantly pushing, reaching, hustling to meet our next target. And the one after that. And the one after that.

BE REASONABLE About the last thing anybody wants is to work for someone who's hard to please, hard to figure, and hard to take. Even worse is to find that your colleagues think of you in just these terms. Approach each situation with care and compassion and you'll be better positioned to respond in a positive manner to even the most negative outcome.

GIVE BACK TO MOVE FORWARD I've always been big on doing the honorable thing and setting things right. It goes back to my parents and the way they lived their lives, the choices they made. Live outside yourself. Connect. In business, relationships are all-important, and those relationships extend beyond your staff to your suppliers, your competitors, your community. Your partners, even. Take care of one to take care of the other.

WALK THAT CERTAIN ROAD I'm not suggesting here that we pursue only opportunities that carry a certain outcome. Life and business are all about risk, and we'll blow it all if we don't take chances. But that doesn't mean we take *every* chance, and it certainly doesn't mean we take them recklessly. There is no such thing as a sure thing, but we need to roll the dice with confidence if we mean to succeed. Cover your bets. Work the odds in your favor. Like your chances. Know that you have chosen the best possible course with the best possible outcome for the best possible reasons.

SPEAK YOUR MIND Make room in your view for second-guessing and other differences of opinion. Consensus building is an essential trait for an effective leader, but a top team player will need to challenge consensus every now and then. Leaders, if you can't sell your idea to your own team, you'll never be able to sell it in the marketplace; and if you can't buy an alternative approach from a whole other perspective, you should probably be in the market for a new perspective of your own.

RALLY YOUR TROOPS In a time of crisis, gather your closest and most trusted advisers and have at it. There's a reason top leaders surround themselves with top people. Put yours to work.

SIX

Playing the Game

If you're going to be thinking anyway,
you might as well think big.

–Donald Trump

S ometimes life throws you a curve.

There I was, slogging through the mess of that fire at the west side property, wondering how I might recover what I'd lost, hassling with claims adjusters and real estate attorneys and figuring some kind of next move, when I received a message from the mother of a friend with an unlikely prospect. She was a talent agent in Chicago, representing children, and an open call had crossed her desk for a network reality show. These open calls had pretty much become the order of the day for talent agents all across the country, but this reality show—or unscripted drama, which I would soon learn was the preferred description—was a little outside the ordinary. This one had nothing to do with relationships, conquering your fears, or conquering your fears of relationships. This one called for young business professionals looking to get a leg up in their careers, and for some reason my friend's mother had thought of me. She actually made me an appointment before even talking to me about it, and since I didn't have anything else on my calendar at that hour I decided to see it through.

I had no idea what to expect, and when I got to the casting location I had no idea what to make of it. I'd never been to one of these open calls before. It's like I'd stumbled onto some other planet, that's how weird and otherworldly the whole thing seemed. The large room was full of men and women, some in business suits and some casually dressed, many of them grouped into small huddles, comparing notes and information. Everyone appeared deadly serious—as if this might not be just the chance of a lifetime but the *last* chance of a lifetime.

When your friend's mother sets you up on an audition, it's a good idea to go for it.

For me, it wasn't much more than a lark, but I listened in to learn what I could, and as I did I thought to myself, Hmmm, this could be interesting.

Apparently, there were a lot of folks thinking much the same, because it turned out there were roughly 215,000 other applicants all around the country, responding to the same call. The show was to be produced by Mark Burnett, the producer of *Survivor*, which was generally regarded as the Trump Tower of reality shows, and was to be hosted by billionaire entrepreneur Donald Trump, generally regarded as the *Survivor* of real estate developers and self-promoting businessmen. Donald Trump is the closest thing to an icon among aspiring entrepreneurs, and his name and back story were compelling magnets to anyone just starting out in business. In some markets, the producers had blanketed local radio stations with ads promising the chance to work with Mr. Trump, and folks just flocked to these open calls as if they were handing out success in twelve-ounce bottles. Many of these people were aspiring actors and actresses as much as they were aspiring businessmen and -women, so for them this was an audition like any other. Most of them, though, were hungry, striving young professionals just like me, determined to chase down every opportunity, no matter how unconventional or far-fetched—hoping, I guess, that the faintest chance to move about in loose proximity to a living-large legacy like Donald Trump was worth the momentary indignity of one of these nationwide open calls.

The show was called *The Apprentice,* and it would be set up like almost every other reality show on television. The finalists would live together in a luxury apartment in New York City. They would lock horns in a variety of staged competitions and face one-by-one elimination on the basis of their performance in those competitions. And since it was ultimately a survival-of-the-shrewdest contest, there would undoubtedly be shifting alliances and subterfuge among the contestants. (These last, I'd also soon learn, were staples of the genre.) By the show's finale, there would be one contestant standing and he or she would win the grand prize—the chance to run one of Donald Trump's companies for one year, at a salary of $250,000.

As reality show premises went, this one was cool—a tried-and-true formula set loose on the American dream and presided over by a living, breathing embodiment of that dream. It actually sounded like something I would watch, so now that I was at the audition, I gave it my best shot and hoped I could be a part of it. I had absolutely no clue what I was doing, but I was doing it just the same. I'd prepared a brief résumé, but I didn't have a head shot or a credit sheet like some of the other "actors" in the room, so I waited until my name was called and sat for my first brief interview and hoped to give these earnest producer-type people what they were looking for.

I began to understand why such auditions were known as cattle calls, but I tried to outshine the rest of the herd. Of course I didn't have the first clue what they were looking for, but at the appointed time I answered their questions honestly and presented myself with the integrity and purpose I display in my career. Plus, I trusted the interview process would filter out the actors, leaving the producers with the best and brightest candidates who could make a genuine contribution to The Trump Organization.

I must have been doing something right, because they kept me around. My first interview led to some more waiting and then a second interview. The lines began to thin, but I was still there, along with a couple of dozen others. A few people came back to talk to me a few times more. Someone from the production team asked me hypothetically if I'd be available to head out to California for another round of interviews, which I took to mean I might survive this first cut and that there was something to be said for being focused and genuine. That, or maybe I fit some demographic they were looking to present to Mark Burnett. Maybe they needed a tall, self-made white midwestern male to counter the variously striped MBA candidates and overly aggressive salespeople. Throughout the entire process, I was keenly aware that this was some strange hybrid of a job interview and a casting call, so I had no real idea about my chances.

I should have liked my chances a whole lot, because I did get selected for that callback in California. They'd winnowed our group from 215,000 down to 50, and now they really checked us out. At one point, I was brought in to meet with

Mark Burnett, the godfather of this operation, and I treated the encounter the same way I would if I had worked my way up from personnel to the CEO in a traditional job interview. Burnett was the one who would make the ultimate decision about who would be on the show, so I knew I would do well to make an impression. I also knew that the only way to make a real impression was to keep doing what I was doing. Unfortunately, I was whisked in and out of his office in under two minutes, during which time I didn't have much of a chance to do anything more than shake the man's hand and mumble a few awkward pleasantries.

Buck convention.

I thought that would be it, the end of my long run in the world of unscripted drama, and I slipped off to lick my wounds, but soon enough fate smiled down and offered me another shot at Mark Burnett. Happily, this time we made a good connection. At least I could hope we had made a good connection. Mark Burnett is an entrepreneur, same as me. He is a hustler, same as me. And he is a stickler for detail, same as me. He is bright, self-effacing, and personable. He'd come to the United States from Australia, by way of England and a stint in the British Royal Army, and somehow wound up selling T-shirts on Venice Beach. He'd even worked as a nanny for a stretch, and after a short time in California he managed to develop and produce the *Eco-Challenge* outdoor adventure competitions for the Discovery Channel. In obvious ways, those shows paved the way for *Survivor*, which became a runaway, industry-transforming hit and changed the very nature of prime time network television.

Not bad for a guy who used to sell T-shirts.

We talked for about an hour on this second pass, and I

came away impressed. This guy Burnett was the real deal. He was passionate about what he was doing and meant to do it better than anybody else—and so far he was doing just that. I could only hope that I made even a slight impression on him, and that he was still looking for that tall, self-made white midwestern male to round out his lineup.

At the end of my five-day "interview," Burnett informed me that I had made his cut. I was in, and thrilled, but the show had almost no public presence whatsoever, which meant that outside the circle of production, no one had really heard of it. I went back to Chicago to wait out the few weeks before taping was to begin in New York. I'd told only a few close friends and family what I had been up to out in Los Angeles, but it was tough for them to get a clear fix on the situation. Hell, it was tough for me to understand what was going on, or what I might or might not be getting myself into, so I tried to concentrate on my building projects and my consultancy work at Cigars Around the World. There was still the pending matter of the fire investigation and the resulting insurance claim, and I was on the hunt for another promising property. The great thing about the cigar business, now that I was out from under and working as a consultant, was that I was free to come and go as I pleased, and as the situation warranted. If there was a crisis, I could be all over it; if there was nothing new, I could be off chasing another opportunity.

Be yourself, no matter what.

During this period I found time to think about why I *really* wanted in on this television show. What had started as a goof was now close enough to taste, and I realized that the experience would be a kind of validation. It would be an adventure, that's for sure, but more than that, it would be a challenge, and a chance to see how my approach to business stacked up against the approaches of a carefully selected group of my peers. I didn't care about any attendant celebrity that might come my way as a result. In truth, I didn't even think about it, that's how naive I was about the whole experience. All it was, really, was the chance to compete against other businessmen and -women, to work alongside an entrepreneurial giant like Donald Trump, to see how my strategies looked when put to the test.

I approached it like a weeks-long seminar that could net me an advanced degree in tactics and strategies. And if I managed to win the whole thing and land the job with The Trump Organization? Well then, that would be a year-long seminar in more of the same, taught by one of the most successful businessmen in the world.

Yes, I got the call that I would appear on the show. Yes, I was energized about meeting Donald Trump and soaking up what I could of his vast experience. (Be the sponge, I kept telling myself. *Be the sponge.*) Yes, I was bursting to tell people about it, even though I didn't know exactly what I would tell them at this point. And yes, I was determined to approach the game as I had approached my life and career.

First thing I had to do was get my life in order so that I could set it aside for a few months. For some folks, I imagine this would have been easier said than done; for me, it was just done. It was late August 2003, and I had about a million things going on, and I was expected to be in New York in just a few weeks for an undetermined stretch that could last as long as two months. I could step away from the cigar business without too much worry, with an invaluable assist from my associate, Jennifer Davenport; and I could put some of my real estate projects on pause and others on a kind of autopilot, with support from my development guru Stuart Miller and my diligent colleague Kathy Nakos, who had provided so much help in the development of that property on the south side. I had things covered in such a way that I wouldn't lose too much in the way of time or ground or money during the run of the show.

On top of everything else, I was contemplating the longest stretch of time I'd ever been away from home. I don't mean to come across as a mama's boy or anything like that, but the truth is I hadn't been away from Chicago or from my family for any longer than a couple of weeks at a time, and here I was looking at displacing myself for two months or more, which meant that on top of everything else, I was also worried about being out of my element.

Television is a funny business, I came to realize. *The Apprentice* wouldn't air until January 2004, but we were taping in the heat of late summer and all through September and October. Every three days we'd be dispatched on a new pressure-filled assignment; we'd have a day or two to plan and a day or two to execute. Typically, there'd be one afternoon or evening to celebrate if you were part of the winning team on any given task, and that same afternoon or evening to lick your wounds if you were part of the losing team. This last would include a boardroom showdown with Donald Trump and two members of his executive team, which would then result in an agonizing confrontation with Mr. Trump to determine which team members would keep their jobs for another round and which would be fired.

> Once your foot is in the door, be sure the rest of you follows.

For dramatic effect as much as for logistical reasons, players on the losing team were made to pack up their belongings from the Trump Tower loft we all shared and to cart them to the boardroom for their moment of reckoning. If you were fired, you were quite literally sent packing, made to leave the building immediately.

It didn't take a genius to figure out that the one sure way to survive on *The Apprentice* was to succeed at each task, this on the theory that if Donald Trump couldn't catch you he couldn't fire you. If your team kept winning each head-to-head competition, you would never face Mr. Trump's axe, so there was every incentive to outperform the other team. However, the downside to this surefire strategy was that the winning team spent hardly any time at all in the Trump boardroom, so they didn't get any benefit from his insight or experience either—at least not in the first several rounds. They were safe, but in the end I'm betting they were also sorry, if the reasons they'd thrown in on this effort had been anything like mine.

There were sixteen finalists at the start of the show. We didn't meet each other until we showed up at Trump Tower to begin taping the first episode, so there was no chance to size each other up or check each other out. We were shown our loft apartment and brought together to receive our first assignment, all in less than an hour. There wasn't even time to unpack.

As we shook hands all around, I realized the producers had done a tremendous job casting us contestants, because there were competitors of every stripe and background. We all had strong personalities, but that's pretty much where our similarities ended. We were shy and retiring and outgoing and brazen. We were funny and serious. We were seat-of-the-pants and thorough; theory and practice; leaders and followers. We were a little bit of everything, but the one constant was this: We were all in our twenties and thirties, all at least somewhat successful in our business ventures to this point, and all hungry to get and keep ahead. We may have thrown in on this reality show venture for a variety of individual reasons, but everyone was on his or her way up, with room to grow and a lot to learn.

Here's a quick rundown of the rest of the field, in no particular order:

Heidi, an account executive in the telecommunications industry from Philadelphia

Tammy, a stockbroker from Seattle

David, a doctor turned MBA turned venture capitalist from New York City

Jason, a real estate developer from Detroit

Ereka, a marketing and sales representative in the cosmetics industry from New York City

Nick, a Xerox salesman from Los Angeles

Jessie, a midwestern realtor who also ran her own chiropractic clinics

Bowie, a commercial real estate broker from Dallas

Kwame, a Harvard MBA, most recently working as an investment banker in New York City

Sam, an Internet entrepreneur from the Washington, DC area

Amy, an MBA working in high-tech consulting from Austin, Texas

Kristi, a restaurateur from Santa Monica, California

Omarosa, a former political consultant from Washington, D.C.

Me with my mom and dad.
(*Inset*) With my three incredibly supportive sisters on my first birthday.

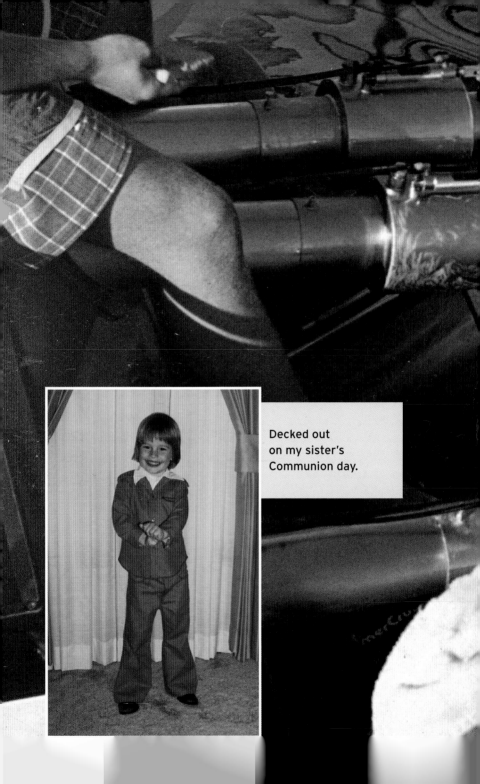

Decked out
on my sister's
Communion day.

Happily working away
on my boat wash and
wax business.

CIGARS
AROUND THE WORLD

Cigars Around the World™ is a full service Cigar distribution and fulfillment company. Since 1993, Cigars Around the World has been providing premium cigars to organizations spanning the globe. We find the rarest cigars from the most unique destinations and guarantee freshness to you. We provide outstanding service from training and set-up through fulfillment and replenishment on a daily basis. Special events, custom orders and specialty cigars are our pleasure at Cigars Around the World. We can even supply the humidor for your locations upon request. As seen on CNN™ and Good Morning America™ Cigars Around the World is the best on-premise cigar fulfillment program in the country. Where there is smoke, there is a buyer. Service, selection and premium style, all with Cigars Around the World. *Contact us today to get rolling.*

I was incredibly proud by the launch of my first business.

World Class

CIGARS
AROUND THE WORLD

1.800.fresh.66

Dad helping me start Cigars Around the World.

Enjoying a quick smoke of cigar success.

There's no greater feeling than having your first office.

Mike Ditka was one of the first guys that supported Cigars Around the World in a big way (my sis was very excited to meet him).

As scary as it was exhilarating, this is the first building I ever bought, developed, and sold.

Constant sources of inspiration: my Mom and my sister Karen.

There are just some things you can't control, like when my second building project burned down. But I never let it stop me from trying again.

Dealing with the media and instant celebrity isn't always easy. (*Inset*) After I won *The Apprentice*, things changed in a big way.

HARRISON'S
RESTAURANT · BREWERY
TRUMPS APPRENTICE BILL
HERE WED JAN 21 7

A great first appearance on *Live with Regis & Kelly*. (*Inset*) My interview with Jen Scheft and Jamie Blyth from *The Bachelorette*.

Troy, a mortgage broker from Boise, Idaho

Katrina, a real estate broker from Miami

Even among a group of strong personalities, some come across more forceful than the rest, and folks very quickly adapted to their new roles within the forced dynamic of the show. Some who might have been outspoken back home and out in front in the career they'd set aside chose to hang back and let others take charge, while others seized the first opportunity to make their marks on this group, on the producers, and on Mr. Trump and his executive team.

In a lot of ways, it was like the first day of summer camp rolled together with the first day of summer internships at a city law firm. Granted, I'd never been to summer camp, and I'd never worked as a summer intern at a city law firm, but I'm guessing that's what it was like. In any case, we were all jockeying for position, sizing each other up, and trying to act natural in a most unnatural situation. Basically, we were trying to come across as confident and competent and competitive, although in actual practice we weren't any of these things, at just that moment—at least not to judge from our out-of-the-gate execution of the show's first task. We were split into two teams, men versus women, and the fact that we cut along gender lines into two equal groups reinforced my suspicions that we were all chosen for this final round for reasons having as much to do with central casting as with our qualifications for a meaningful role within The Trump Organization.

The women chose a name for their team—Protégé, which I thought was strong and sharp.

We men chose a name for our team—VersaCorp, which I thought left a little something to be desired.

Our first assignment: to sell lemonade on the streets of New York City. It was, from a storyboard standpoint, an ideal introductory task. It was Business 101, the fundamentals of supply and demand and location and strategy, all mixed together in an under-the-gun way that would let each group flourish or flounder, depending on our abilities to work as a team. And it gave each individual a chance, on the simplest scale, to put his or her business skills to the test. Each team had a budget to cover the cost of supplies (cups, lemonade mix, water), a team leader (or project manager) to oversee the group's efforts, and a set time frame in which to generate as much money from sales as possible. Indeed, most every task on the show would be determined in a quantifiable way—sales, receipts, head counts . . . some measure to separate the winners from the losers. Note here that the task was not to sell the most lemonade in that given period of time, but to earn the most money doing it—a distinction that would leave Sam, our decidedly outlandish Internet entrepreneur, trying to sell a single glass for as much as $1,000.

> Check your ego at the door and assume the other guy has checked his as well.

The wrinkle to this first task was that only a few of us knew Manhattan well enough to come up with a suitable location for our lemonade stands, which left the rest of us scrambling to understand our market. (And which left us men doing our ill-conceived selling at the South Street Seaport, awash in the stink of fresh seafood.) I don't think either team performed all that well, in large part because we were still getting to know each other and our assorted strengths and weaknesses, and also because we were slow to grasp that we were embarking on a competition that was more of a game than a job interview. However, I don't intend to offer a blow-by-blow or play-by-play account of each week's task or of the twists and turns of the competition. All of that made for fascinating television, but I don't think it would make for compelling reading—especially for those of you unfamiliar with the show. Suffice it to say that the women of Protégé kicked our butts that first time out—and the second, third, and fourth times, too. We guys on the VersaCorp team saw a whole lot of Mr. Trump's boardroom those first few episodes, that's for sure, and after four firings our ranks were so severely depleted the producers had to shed the men versus women angle to keep the teams balanced.

Turn fear into focus.

I'll leave the show-by-show analysis to someone else and focus instead on the tasks that did a lot of business for me personally as a candidate for the Trump job—and a lot of business for the show in general with the way they crystallized what the competition was really about.

For the second task, down to fifteen contestants, we were whisked to the cutting-edge offices of advertising impresario Donny Deutsch and charged with dreaming up a print ad campaign for Marquis Jet, a Deutsch client looking to establish its private jet leasing business. This would be one of the few assignments where the teams would be judged on something other than mere numbers; Donny Deutsch would consider our completed campaigns, consult with his agency colleagues and with Mr. Trump, and determine a winner.

It was an exciting challenge, and both teams set about it with some inspired bits of creativity and vision. The women of Protégé came up with a racy, risky approach, suggestively using the airplane as a phallic symbol and generally playing to an audience of men who might associate a private jet with issues of power and virility. It was a bold move, built on the accepted notion that sex sells and highlighting one of the distinct advantages enjoyed by the Protégé team during the first leg of the competition. We were all super-competitive, but there was no competing with the fact that they were a whole lot prettier than we were and that their looks couldn't help but come into play in one way or another.

We men of VersaCorp took a more conservative approach, focusing instead on the safety and comfort of private jet travel and highlighting the status of being able to afford it. There was nothing bold about our effort, but it was a smart, polished campaign we all thought would play well in our pitch.

However, the VersaCorp team made a critical error. We neglected to meet with the heads of the Marquis Jet company or with head of the advertising agency to determine what the client was looking to accomplish with this campaign, where their tastes and sensibilities lay, and who their target audience might be. A group of us pushed aggressively to set up these key meetings, but Jason, our project manager, determined that there simply wasn't enough time to take these meetings and still polish our print campaign. He was right that there was a significant time crunch, but to my thinking, nothing was more important than meeting with the client. That should have been our first step, but we were so intimidated by our deadline that we chose instead to scramble without a clear goal in mind.

The women of Protégé knew better. They set up strategy meetings with Marquis Jet executives and Donny Deutsch and his agency team and were therefore able to produce edgy material that stayed within the bounds of what the client was comfortable with, while we played it safe to cover the fact that we had no idea what the client would be comfortable with.

Put another way, the women did their homework while the dog ate ours.

Predictably, the Protégé team won this round, and Jason wound up taking the fall for the guys because it was his decision not to meet with the client—a crucial mistake that cost him a chance to advance in the competition.

For the eighth episode, now down to nine contestants after a variety of assignments that had us doing everything from running a flea market to leasing a luxury loft space to selecting and promoting a contemporary artist in a downtown gallery opening, we were dispatched with a couple of truckloads of Trump Ice, an upstart, upmarket brand of bottled water featuring our host and spirit guide on the label. The teams had been shuffled by this point, and Ereka was the project manager for my group, which also included Nick and Katrina. Unlike the more subjective advertising task, this one would once again come down to the numbers, so we blanketed the city with our sales efforts and hoped like heck we could sell more water than Heidi, Troy, Omarosa, Kwame, and Amy.

> Always keep an open line of communication with partners and clients.

Given our limited time frame, it made sense to try to write the biggest possible orders—selling multiple cases by the pallet or the truckload, if at all possible—but we were handicapped in this effort by the limited storage space available to most midtown restaurants and convenience stores. Refrigeration space wasn't an issue, because the water only needed to be *served* cold and could be stored at room temperature, but most outlets simply didn't have the room to accommodate the kinds of substantial orders we were looking to write. Most weren't willing to write a long-term, open-ended purchase order that would have allowed us to count those future sales in our one-day total. We might have anticipated as much going in, but once we started to notice the trend we began to rethink our strategy. I imagine the other team was coming up against the same barriers in their efforts and adjusting their own plan accordingly. Even when we were able to find someone willing to take on the product, they would buy only a few cases at a time, wanting to see how their customers responded to the new product, and we all knew that to outpace the competition we needed to make a bigger hit. We looked to distributors and wholesalers, to try to generate more substantive sales, but typically these outlets already carried several bottled waters and couldn't be persuaded to take on a new line.

Here again, the task turned on the project manager's approach, reinforcing the theory that it's lonely at the top and that the buck has got to stop somewhere. Ereka was all caught up in the glitz and glamour associated with the Trump name, which I guess is understandable considering that we were living in the Trump Tower and enjoying the perks that came with that lifestyle. In her sales pitches, she kept referring to the great buzz the water would generate among customers, or the luster that might come their way by sipping from the Trump well. Time after time the restaurant managers or buyers couldn't understand why they should care about buzz or luster as it related to bottled water. After all, bottled waters are all pretty much the same, and the only real concern these people had was how much the stuff was going to cost and how much they could sell it for. Everything else was just salesmanship.

On my own sales calls, I tried to emphasize the competitive pricing I was able to offer and presented potential buyers with a thoughtful plan. I spoke to them in their language. They didn't care about the allure of the Trump name or any presumed association with the Trump brand, so I didn't bother them with it. As far as they were concerned, the name was irrelevant, so I came in with all kinds of spreadsheets and scenarios, depending on the type and size of the operation, letting the numbers make the sale rather than a slick pitch. And it worked. I couldn't say for sure what Nick, Katrina, and Ereka were doing on their own individual sales calls, but I was able to move a lot of water using this approach.

Once again, my team came up short, and here Ereka's critical mistake came in laying blame. In all fairness, she had to point fingers somewhere; that was the nature of the game. I simply questioned the direction in which she chose to point. After each task, the losing project manager would summon two team members to the boardroom with him or her to confront Mr. Trump. It was entirely the project manager's call who would join them in the firing line. The other team members would be spared and automatically advanced to the next round. For some reason, Ereka chose to take me and Nick into the boardroom with her, even though I had sold more cases of water than anyone on our team, and Nick had contributed substantially to our effort as well.

This was one of those textbook examples of a personal relationship clouding a professional judgment. Ereka and

Katrina had grown close during those first weeks of taping. They were almost like sisters, and when Ereka had a chance to spare her friend a possible firing she sent Katrina back to the safety of our loft and dragged Nick and me to the boardroom. Mr. Trump and his executive team couldn't understand her decision. Actually, let me amend this point, because of course they could *understand* it. The friendship between Ereka and Katrina was clear to everyone involved with the show. What they couldn't do was justify it, so they asked Ereka to do it for them.

Mr. Trump turned to Ereka and put it plainly: "Why isn't Katrina in here with you?" he asked, already knowing the answer.

Ereka fumbled and said something about how she couldn't see what Katrina was doing throughout the entire task, so therefore she couldn't exactly blame her for the team's shortfall.

> Do your job and do it well, and let your work speak for itself. Leave the office politicking to folks who need to call attention to their efforts.

It was clear to all of us in that room that Ereka was simply covering for her friend, but in trying to spare Katrina she ended up costing herself a shot at the top job. Someone had to be fired, and Mr. Trump couldn't see firing our team's two top producers, so Ereka was sent packing—sending a lesson to the rest of us and soon enough to our millions of television viewers that business and friendships are indeed a dangerous mix.

For the next challenge, down to eight contestants, we were set loose on the city streets with our own fleet of petty cabs—bicycle-pulled rickshaws. As a mode of transportation, the things fell somewhere between a taxi and a horse-drawn carriage in terms of cost and tourist-friendly photo opportunities, and most of our potential customers were clustered around the great hotels off Central Park South and the midtown stretches of Fifth Avenue. The teams were given a day to strategize, followed by an eight-hour shift in which to operate, at the end of which the team generating the most revenues would be declared the winner.

Now, I happened to be the project manager for my team this time out, and to my thinking the winner of this competition would not be determined by fares alone. The average ride pulled about $5 to $10, and we could keep our rickshaws fully loaded and operational the entire eight hours and still never crack four figures. The thing to do was to look at ways to maximize the return on our efforts—to "sell the sawdust," to revisit that phrase from my buddy Carson Sterling in the lumberyard business. We need look no further than the ads billboarded to the doors and hoods of every cab in the city, or the commercial flyers I used to insert in the packages of cigars I shipped each month to my club members, for a ready solution to the task at hand: advertising. We could sell ad space on the sides of the rickshaws, which would be pedaled around the city's busiest streets at the busiest time of day, where there was a high concentration of pedestrian traffic, tourists, and window shoppers. When the notion hit, it reminded me of the way NASCAR drivers sell every inch of space on their jumpsuits and helmets and cars to motor oil and tire companies, so I figured if it could work on a big scale in a sustained way, the concept would also work on this quick-hit one-shot basis.

Because this was the tenth task set before us, we had already established a great many contacts in and around the city. They knew us, they knew Donald Trump, and they knew the show. There was the Marquis Jet company for which we had dreamed up that ill-conceived advertising concept, art galleries where we had displayed the works of two up-and-coming artists, a Planet Hollywood restaurant in Times Square that we had taken turns managing for one evening, and any number of restaurants where we had eaten as a large group in the context of the show. And just why were these relationships important? Well, at Cigars Around the World, I was always reaching back to folks I'd done business with, just to check in and reinforce the contact, on the theory that you never know when you'll need to call on someone again. I made it a point to always end each business association on a positive note, and I continued this practice during each of our tasks on the show, which meant that we had a ready base of potential advertisers who already knew who we were and what we were about. True, we could have cold-called any restaurateur in the city or any manufacturer or service provider, pitching the same advertising concept, but we would have had to spend all that extra time explaining why there was a camera crew tailing our every move, and why we could run their ads for only one eight-hour shift, and why we were willing to stay up half the night designing and printing the ads ourselves at Kinko's. As Ricky Ricardo would say, that was an awful lot of 'splainin' to do.

It was a better use of our limited time, we thought, to reach first to our area contacts and hope we could sell through our ad space in this way—and as hard sells went, it wasn't all that hard. The one snag was determining a fair advertising rate, not so steep that it would turn off a potential advertiser who understood the concept, and not so cheap that it wouldn't assure us a victory. By the end of our first strategy day we had secured deals that would blanket our entire fleet with display advertising for the next day's shift, and as we closed the last of these deals we all felt sure we were on to a winning strategy. The two women on our team even agreed to don T-shirts and hats with a relevant corporate logo in order to cement the agreement with the corporate jet leasing company, when it was suggested by one of the Marquis Jet executives that pretty girls wearing his branded clothing would be an effective selling strategy.

The hardest part of this task was designing and printing the ads and figuring out how to secure them to the rickshaws in such a way that they could withstand the potholes of the city streets and the jostling of countless customers and passersby. Some of us were up all night long putting the finishing touches on these things, but when your team is down to just four people it's a hands-on operation all around. I'm big on delegating, but there has to be someone to delegate *to*, wouldn't you agree?

The one speed bump to our strategy came in the form of a moral dilemma. At some point during our eight-hour shift the next day, a sign promoting a midtown restaurant fell off one of our rickshaws. It took a while before any of us noticed it, and by that point the advertiser had missed out on a good chunk of his paid-for advertising time—time that was essentially irretrievable, since we were only operating for this one eight-hour shift. The honorable thing to do was go back to the restaurateur before the day was through and offer him some kind of rebate for the time lost. The dilemma came in how much of a rebate to offer. Our team was fairly split on how to handle this. Some in our group felt strongly that we should give this guy a full refund, since we had failed to deliver on our promise. I was of the opinion that we should offer only a partial rebate, perhaps on a prorated basis, because the advertiser certainly received some value for his unconventional media buy. The day hadn't been a total bust. Of course, when you factored in the windfall television coverage he received when we returned to his establishment to negotiate a settlement, he had made one of the all-time media buys in advertising history, but we tried not to factor the windfall television coverage into the equation.

Keep your word and you will keep your contacts.

As it happened, though, the team member we dispatched to handle the settlement believed that the only appropriate response was to refund the entire fee—a move that might have made sense if we were in a long-term business, hoping to build a long-term relationship with this advertiser and to establish our credibility going forward. Under these circumstances it seemed only to cut our cushion out from under us. We do the right thing by degrees, I remember thinking at the time, and here we might have gone a little beyond the parameters of the right thing.

Still, even with this unexpected giveback, we all felt there was enough cushion left to outearn the other team—which we did, by an overwhelming margin—and at the end of this particular day I felt particularly gratified, because after all the other hoops we had been made to jump through, this was really the first time Donald Trump would have reason to take note of my contributions. My fingerprints were all over this good result. I was drawing on the creative instincts that had built Cigars Around the World from a notion into a viable brand. This was me, as project manager, demonstrating my ability to lead and motivate and deliver on the back of a brainstorm. I was standing boldly behind a bright idea and working it to full effect.

If the format of the show entitled each one of us surviving deep into the contest a defining moment of one kind or another, then surely this had been mine, so I chalked it up to a meaningful experience and looked ahead to the next task, and the one after that, and the one after that.

In the twelfth challenge, the six surviving contestants traveled to the Trump Taj Mahal in Atlantic City to sign up as many high rollers as we could in a kind of frequent gamblers promotion being run at the casino. Guests could sign up for a Taj Mahal card that would earn them credits for gifts and vouchers from casino merchants depending on how much and how frequently they gambled. We were to register as many of these card holders as we could in a set period.

Once again, we would be judged by how much our total pool of gamblers wagered over that period of time, not on how many gamblers we were able to sign up, so it was all about quality and not quantity. A small number of high rollers could easily outwager a greater number of small-stakes gamblers during the specified time, so I immediately set my sights on the VIPs who could win this competition for us with some big-time bets. As it turned out, I was essentially alone in this strategy—at least at the outset.

I was working with Kwame and Troy on this one, and we managed to secure a wheel-of-fortune type roulette wheel from the casino's prop department, which we outfitted to feature special giveaway items to lure card members to our effort. The idea was to get them to register with us in exchange for a spin at the wheel, which offered the chance at some cold, hard cash—which, after all, was why everyone was in town in the first place.

Amy, Nick, and Katrina hit on their own giveaway promotion, making arrangements with a local car dealer to provide a free luxury rental to one of their winners. On the surface, there was a lot of sizzle to the other team's concept, because it allowed them to roll out a hot car onto the floor outside the casino, but there wasn't a lot of steak to it because it was hard to get people excited about a rental—even a multiday rental of a luxury car. All day long, in fact, you could see folks flocking to the other team's booth and to their car, only to come away disappointed once they realized it wasn't the car itself that was actually up for grabs but the chance to borrow it for a couple days.

Troy and Kwame made arrangements for some of the exotic animals from one of the Taj Mahal shows to be caged alongside our prize wheel, in hopes of luring customers to sign in with us—and it seemed like a good idea at the time. Like Las Vegas, Atlantic City is all about bells and whistles, and the tigers and lions would be a powerful lure, so we were all excited about this concept when it first alighted.

While Troy and Kwame were busy with their exotic animals, I set my sights on even bigger game—at the hotel's VIP check-in desk. The night before the competition, when each team was plotting its strategy, I requested a copy of the VIP manifest from the hotel manager, which included a detailed accounting of each guest's betting history at the Taj Mahal and projections of what they would likely wager on this next visit. Such manifests, I learned, are standard stuff at most top hotel-casinos, and I was merely taking full advantage of the information available to our hotel colleagues. With the manifest in hand, I was then able to negotiate an exclusive arrangement with the manager at the VIP check-in desk, allowing me to personally greet each high roller upon check-in and welcome him or her to the casino with a small gift—a bar of gourmet chocolate, which I purchased in bulk using some of my team's seed money. Once I had their attention and welcomed them to the hotel on behalf of The Trump Organization, I invited these VIP players to take a spin at our cash wheel and swipe their Taj Mahal card with our group.

In actual practice, the exclusive arrangement was little more than a nod of permission from the VIP manager after I'd explained the service I wanted to offer these customers, but it still gave us a great corner on a key segment of our target market and an all-important edge over our competition. I felt certain that for every one VIP I managed to check in the other team would have to register a dozen or so regular players just to keep pace.

I'm not sure Kwame and Troy saw the vision and wisdom in my efforts, because there wasn't room in theirs for much beyond the lions and tigers. Kwame was the project manager for our team, and he and Troy were pumped over these animals. I had to hand it to them—when the exotic animal handlers rolled those cages out onto the floor outside the casino where we had set up our wheel, the animals generated a great deal of excitement. Unfortunately, the excitement quickly turned out to be more of a distraction than a draw, as hotel and casino guests wandered by to see what all the fuss was about and couldn't be bothered to spin our wheel or register their Taj Mahal cards with us. We got a lot of attention, but not a whole lot of business.

> **D**on't be afraid to make a bold move. Just be sure you can back it up.

Still, with two-thirds of our team focused on the animals and the wheel, the exotic animal push represented the bulk of our ongoing efforts, so I guess you could say I went rogue on my team. I had an idea and went with it—even without the full endorsement of my project manager. Kwame knew what I was up to, and I had his tacit approval to see it through, but I had the sense all day long that he felt I should have been out there on the floor with him and Troy.

At some point, Amy sparked to what I was doing over at the VIP check-in counter, and she dispatched one of the hostesses her team had hired to help them greet guests and sign them up to their side. These hostesses were attractive local models, and I made the great mistake of calling them hookers in front of the television cameras. I realize now that this didn't exactly endear me to millions of viewers and probably wasn't the smoothest move in the history of prime time television, but I resented the fact that these scantily dressed women were sent to hone in on my turf. This was a classy operation catering to a classy clientele, and I'd been conducting what I hoped was a classy, personal greeting effort, and here these showgirls were dispatched to pull these big-time players in another direction. It was amateurish, a clownish tug-of-war for business, and it made all of us look bad. I even thought it made the Taj Mahal look bad, and I said as much. After some back-and-forth with Amy I was able to push her hostesses from the VIP area and back to the other team's side of the lobby.

At the end of the day, our group registered about 700 players, to roughly 1,400 checked in by the other team. In terms of raw numbers, we were screwed. But remember, it was all about the quality of the players we signed on, not the quantity, and our group "outgambled" the other group by about a 50 percent margin—validating my theory on pursuing these VIPs.

The victory was especially sweet because it reinforced for me the importance of following my own instincts even when those went somewhat against the rest of the room. In truth, it's not like I went against Kwame in focusing on this high-end group, it's just that I stuck to my hunches, and in business you sometimes have to go with your gut to get ahead.

In the end, by design or coincidence, it came down to a contest between book smarts and street smarts: Kwame Jackson, the Wall Street investment banker, versus yours truly. The Harvard MBA versus the seat-of-the-pants entrepreneur. The ivory tower versus the real world. I don't think producer Mark Burnett or the NBC promotional team could have scripted a better showdown for their unscripted drama. It was the classic business dichotomy, played out on prime time television, and it would push Donald Trump to weigh theory versus practice.

I liked Kwame a great deal and couldn't overestimate his abilities. He was smooth and analytical and insightful. He was a sound team player and a thoughtful team leader. Most noticeably, he carried himself on the show with the kind of quiet cool that set him apart from the other players and positioned him as a confident manager with an innate ability to troubleshoot problems without breaking a sweat. To his discredit, I should point out, it was Kwame who came up with the bright idea of setting up our lemonade stand by the fish market, a miscalculation of a first impression it seemed Donald Trump would never let him live down, and over the run of the show he appeared to have to troubleshoot more than his fair share of problems, which is never a good sign if you mean to position yourself as an effective leader.

For example, in the final head-to-head task, Kwame was sent back down to Atlantic City, where he was put in charge of a Jessica Simpson concert at the Taj Mahal. I headed north, to the Trump National Golf and Country Club in Westchester County, to manage a celebrity golf tournament. We had a chance to pick our own teams for support, and here Kwame made what I thought at the time was a key mistake. He selected Troy, Heidi, and Omarosa, the very same team he had been beaten badly with in one of the earlier rounds, and try as I might I couldn't understand his thinking. I mean, if a strategy backfires the first time around, what kind of leader goes back to the same strategy a second time?

Even worse for Kwame, I thought, was how he handled his team—specifically, how he handled Omarosa, who had turned out to be a handful. She was deceitful, disorganized, and completely unprofessional, but Kwame let each of her transgressions slide. I don't know if he was just trying to be a good guy or if he didn't have it in him to take charge. At one point, the cameras caught Omarosa in a brazen lie, and at another she was spotted modeling outfits with Jessica Simpson when she had been sent to deliver the star to a meet-and-greet audience event. He should have fired her, a bold move that would have made a tremendous impression on the no-nonsense Mr. Trump. When Kwame was later called on this, he said he wasn't aware that he could do such a thing. What kind of leader lets an incompetent, insubordinate member of his team put such a drag on his chances?

> Things change, and so should your ability to adapt to any situation.

For my part, the charity golf tournament went off without any major hitches, and I seemed to handle the minor ones effectively, so I was liking my chances in the competition, at least insofar as these final tasks would determine the outcome. Clearly, Mr. Trump would look to our performances during the run of the show in making his decision on who to hire and who to fire, and he would look as well to how we handled ourselves in the upcoming final boardroom session.

I cast myself as an underdog and determined to come out fighting. A lot of people kept telling me that a guy like Donald Trump would almost certainly be drawn to a scrappy, self-made businessman over a polished investment banker type, but I couldn't count on almost. In making such a public hire, even if it was an elaborate publicity stunt, Mr. Trump would also be making a public statement, and I didn't see it as a sure thing that he would come down on one side or the other. He could reach for the guy who most reminded him of himself at a younger age, or he could reach for the guy with the slick academic pedigree he might have always wished he had. It was a tough call, all around.

In my head, I ran through all kinds of scenarios and mock boardroom sessions, looking to build up my confidence and to develop a game plan as we approached the final "live" boardroom showdown. All along, throughout the run of the show, I'd tried to avoid pointing fingers at my teammates when a task didn't go well, and judging from the message board responses on the NBC website, this didn't always go over so great with viewers handicapping my chances. It was a damned-if-you-do, damned-if-you-don't situation. If I spoke out against a member of my own team, I was perceived as disloyal. If I spoke in favor of a member of my own team, I was perceived as lying or posturing or currying support from that team member in return. If I chose to stay out of the fray, I was perceived as being indecisive. I couldn't win for trying with these people, but at this late stage I'd have to rethink my approach. At this point, I realized I'd have to come out firing—acknowledging Kwame's strong suits, perhaps, but highlighting the holes in his game. Leo "The Lip" Durocher, the former Cubs manager and a Chicago sports legend, was famous for his statement that nice guys finish last, and in this situation I looked for a way to continue to play nice, to maintain my integrity and still manage to come out ahead.

I realized too that if I took a totally positive approach—that is, if I was unwilling to point out any of Kwame's negatives or criticize any of his initiatives—I would always be on the defensive. This was a competition, after all, and I would have to come out swinging if I hoped to stand any kind of chance. Obviously, I would try to trumpet my own abilities without smearing my opponent, but in our previous boardroom sessions Mr. Trump had made it a special point of asking each of us to address the failings of our colleagues. He struck me as a tell-it-like-it-is guy, and I would have to figure a way to offer honest, objective criticism without having it come across as sniping or finger-pointing.

The key would be to position myself as a capable generalist, able to get along in virtually any business setting, and to remind Mr. Trump that I'd hired, trained, motivated, and terminated more people than anyone else among the sixteen finalists who started this competition. About the best line I came up with was this, to deflect the theoretical value of Kwame's Harvard MBA over my bachelor's degree from Loyola: "Mr. Trump, with all due respect, MBAs like Kwame go to work for guys like you and me who start companies. We make job offers to guys like Kwame. He chose to work for someone else. I chose to start, grow, and manage my own business. If you want someone to manage and grow your company, I'm your man. Then if we choose to sell the business, we can hire Kwame."

When game day finally rolled around the calendar, I was ready. Here again, there are no surprises in this retelling. The boardroom discussion didn't exactly follow the script I'd developed in my head, but it covered some of the ground, and I was able to shine a positive light on some of my accomplishments while at the same time questioning some of Kwame's decisions during the competition and his abilities going forward. And at the other end of a fairly tense back-and-forth, in front of a live studio audience and 40 million Americans watching at home, Donald Trump turned to me and uttered the two little words all sixteen finalists had been longing to hear, all those months ago: "You're hired."

Then he gave me my first assignment. Actually, to be entirely accurate, he gave me a choice of my first assignment, but I would have to choose immediately and get started on it first thing in the morning. In any case, it was during that moment—shot through with pandemonium and purpose—that I realized just what it was that set Donald Trump apart from most other businessmen, and just what it would take to discover something of the same in myself. He doesn't sit still long enough for the dust to settle. He's all business all the time, all the way. He's always moving, always thinking, always taking charge, and if I meant to keep up with him for the next year I would have to do the same. And as the band played and the crowd roared and my mother and sisters started to cry at the sheer surprise and thrill of it all and the NBC executives and members of Mark Burnett's production team spilled out onto the stage to celebrate a ridiculously successful first season, I thought, Here I go.

Lessons Learned
ON EXECUTION

MAKE A DECISION The ability to achieve consensus will be a hallmark of your leadership skills, but an effective team leader needs to put his or her neck on the line from time to time. In his autobiography, former Chrysler head Lee Iacocca remarked that the most important decisions facing a company are those made by individuals, not committees. Good business instincts can't be taught, and they shouldn't be watered down by a committee. Blind consensus is the absence of leadership. A good leader considers the opinions of others but is not bound by them.

JUST DO IT *Practical execution* is one of the great corporate buzz phrases of my generation, and I'm all over it in my own career. Either you're in it to win it or you're coattailing. If there's a task at hand, the surest way to see it through is to start in on it. Move forward. Make progress every day. Whatever it is, whatever it takes. The guy who drags his feet slows down the entire operation (and kicks up way more dust than absolutely necessary). Get it done—practically, logically, purposefully—and move on.

TAKE ON THE DIFFICULT ASSIGNMENTS You have to be willing to do what others are not. If a thing needs doing, and there's no one better or even comparably suited to the task, then take one for the team. After all, you can't call yourself a team player if you limit your efforts to what comes easy. Go above and beyond and your colleagues will follow.

STYLE COUNTS And so does degree of difficulty. Achieving success in corporate America is a lot like achieving success in ice skating or platform diving at the Olympics. The judges (or bosses) expect you to carry out your routine with precision, but it's what you do underneath, on top of, and all around that precision that sets you apart. Put your own flourish to whatever it is you do. Make a strong first impression and follow it up with a second and third. Make your mark.

SWEAT THE DETAILS, BUT DON'T SWEAT THE OUT-COME There's only so much you can do, and you certainly can't control everything. Do what you can and hope for the best. Put your best foot forward and outpace the strides made by everyone else. If it's out of your control, it's out of your control. Turn your negative energies into positive thinking, and shift your focus to a positive task.

STRIKE FIRST Move quickly, with the confidence to know that even if you haven't figured out all the details, you will. Entrepreneurs are comfortable building the car as they're careening down the road at 100 mph. Also-rans are fumbling through the glove compartment looking for the manual, hoping to find an eject button to propel them to safety.

THINK OUTSIDE THE BOX Another great buzz phrase, but there's some sting to this one too. Sometimes you simply have to reinvent the wheel if you want to push the envelope. I can't stress this enough, yet I'm constantly meeting people who are stymied by the challenge of a new approach. That's probably because they don't recognize the box. Here's one way to go about it. List ten problems in your industry that need to be addressed. Next, list ten accepted or conventional approaches that might have led to those problems. And finally, list ten concepts that are directly opposed to these conventions and craft strategies to employ them. Without even realizing it, you'll have identified the box and lifted your thinking from within it. You *can* build a better mousetrap; all you have to do is think to try.

THINK LIKE AN ASTRONAUT Failure is not an option. Jim Lovell wouldn't accept it during his aborted Apollo 13 mission, when his spacecraft lost contact with NASA beyond the Earth's orbit and was running perilously low on fuel and hope, and neither should you. Refuse to lose. Don't even think about it.

MEET YOUR DEADLINES Nothing succeeds like a schedule. And more to the point, nothing succeeds like a schedule kept. In some businesses, there's a domino effect if you miss your delivery date. One department is kept waiting on another, which in turn is waiting on a third department, and nothing gets done in the downtime. If at all possible, don't set a deadline you're not sure you can meet, but if that's not happening go ahead and set it anyway. And *then* make sure you meet it.

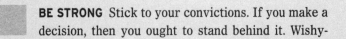

BE STRONG Stick to your convictions. If you make a decision, then you ought to stand behind it. Wishy-washy doesn't cut it even in the detergent business. That said, it doesn't mean you shouldn't sometimes *rethink* a decision if all the signs indicate you've got your people headed the wrong direction. Be prepared to admit a mistake. Yes, if you believe in a plan of attack you need to see it through, even against the best advice of your best colleagues. Own your decisions at the outset, but disown them if and when you must.

GIVE THE CUSTOMER WHAT HE WANTS It's one of the oldest adages in the corporate handbook, but it's no knee-jerk sentiment. You can't expect to make a sale on *your* terms simply because you've got a quota to meet or a boss to satisfy. You've got to convince your customer there's something in it for him, and make the sale on *his* terms. When the women of Protégé took the time to meet with the client before designing and executing an ad campaign for its corporate jet leasing company, they had a clear idea of the client's needs, whereas the men didn't take the time and were flying blind. Conversely, when we were dispatched to sell cases of Trump Ice bottled water to New York City vendors and restaurateurs, one of my colleagues kept pushing the merits of the Trump name on her targeted buyer. It was, I thought, a misguided approach, which was why I made a more direct pitch. I focused on the great price I was able to offer, and the great profit margins that lay in wait, and in this way was able to move more product.

IT'S JUST BUSINESS I don't know if the line is original to Mr. Trump, but it was all over the bumpers for the show when it started to air: "It isn't personal, it's just business." The successful leader is able to separate one from the other. The case of Ereka and Katrina was a text-book example of what can happen when a personal friend-ship gets in the way of a sound management decision. Office friendships can be a tremendous positive, but if they begin to cloud your judgment they might not be worth the trouble. Proceed with caution.

BE TRUE TO YOUR VALUES You have to stand for something or you'll fall for anything. Establish your convictions and have the courage to stand behind them. And while we're on the subject, remember that courage is like a muscle—the more you use it, the stronger it gets.

DRAW FROM A BOTTOMLESS RESERVOIR OF GOOD-WILL Make good on your promises, even if it cuts into your bottom line. A successful outcome is no success at all if there's no one left to call on to help you repeat that success a second time. Or a third.

HATE TO LOSE I know a ton of smart, talented, successful people who look on business as a competitive sport. For every winner, they maintain, there has to be a loser, and these folks owe their various successes to never coming up short. If you're the competitive type, there is merit to this approach. It stands to reason that if your company gains market share, it comes at some other company's expense. And it further stands that if you continually lose market share you'll eventually find yourself out of a job. Transfer your competitive juices from the field to the field office and thrill to the results. If you're not the competitive type, you might try flaring your nostrils just the same. Even the *appearance* of a little fire in the belly couldn't hurt.

KEEP FLUID Perhaps I'm repeating myself here, but I prefer to think of it as reinforcing an all-important point. As essential tools go, agility is right up there. Without it, Cigars Around the World would have gone up in smoke when ad rates ran away from our budget; with it, we were able to reinvent ourselves and carry on. And while you're at it, do your reinventing from a place of real discovery. Make the same mistake twice and you won't get a third chance to do the same.

KEEP IT REAL And keep it realistic. If you've done a deal that no longer makes sense, put it back on the table. Your opposite number can often be made to see things your way if you can help them to see how your position has changed.

BE HUMBLE Don't take your success for granted, but do take it in stride. Nobody likes a braggart or a blowhard, particularly in the workplace, so make the extra effort to wear your accomplishments with grace and humility. If you approach success like you have it coming, it will look the other way; welcome it like a sweet surprise and it just might stick around.

TALK A GOOD GAME Think on the fly. Claim the hot seat as if it were the most comfortable seat in the room. Respond with poise and confidence to every challenge. In Mr. Trump's final boardroom session, I knew I'd be judged as much by my body language as by anything I actually said, so I really had to own my full opinion of myself and my abilities. If I hedged, it would be obvious that I was hedging—which despite Kwame's ineffectiveness during his final challenge could be my ruin.

S E V E N
Putting It All Together

Even great towers start at ground level.
—Chinese proverb

Like most of Donald Trump's real estate properties, the Trump International Tower in the heart of downtown Chicago will be an architectural wonder and a magnificent spectacle upon its completion in 2007. It will feature breathtaking condominium residences, a luxurious world-class hotel, fine restaurants, designer shops and boutiques, and virtually every amenity known to man. At ninety stories, and situated on the current site of the *Sun-Times* headquarters building, fat in the middle of the Gold Coast along the river, it will reinvent the local skyline. And at a projected cost of over $800 million, it is one of the most expensive and extensive building projects the city has ever seen.

I could think of no bigger challenge than to help oversee this project on behalf of The Trump Organization, so when it was presented to me as a possible next career move at the conclusion of *The Apprentice* I grabbed at it. It was a simple decision, really, but it was made inside the excitement, pandemonium, and craziness of prime time network television, in front of more than 40 million viewers. Yet my head was completely clear on this. Mr. Trump gave me the choice of being part of the team that would build this high-rise tower or running his luxury golf course community in Los Angeles. A lot of people might have obsessed over which option made the most sense, but for me there was only one choice: Chicago.

There was every reason to take my career to the next level in the very place it began. Really, the pull was enormous. My family and friends were all in Chicago, along with the White Sox and Cubs and deep-dish pizza and some of the best blues clubs in the country. I wouldn't have to relocate, reacclimate, or otherwise start over. As important, I already had a strong network of business contacts there, particularly in the area of real estate, and some ongoing business interests that would be easier to manage locally than long distance. I knew the city. I knew the streets. I knew how to get around. I knew how to maneuver through the mess of city ordinances and zoning codes.

The Trump International Tower was a daunting project, to be sure, a thousand times bigger than any development project I had yet undertaken and probably a hundred times more than I could handle on my own, but all I could think during that long commercial break on that live NBC soundstage in New York was that one day I'd be able to drive around Chicago with my kids and point to the skyline and the Trump International Tower and say, "Hey, I built that." It was the same juice that had pushed me from cigars into real estate.

And so Chicago it was, and as soon as the live broadcast concluded and the buzz had died down, Mr. Trump pulled me over for a brief private moment and whispered, "You made the right choice." He said he thought there were a few candidates from the show who might have chosen the Los Angeles job, especially those with Hollywood aspirations, but his gut told him I'd opt for the Chicago assignment. "It's a much more interesting project," he said.

I felt sure he was right.

My apprenticeship began the very next morning, although not quite in the ways I had imagined. In The Trump Organization, I would quickly learn, there is no such thing as a predictable routine. No one day is quite like another. And there's no resting on your laurels,

> If you're lucky enough to have the full attention of an expert in your field, take full advantage.

either. Success in one venture is meaningful only if it leads to an even bigger success in the next venture, and now that I was on the payroll, my very first job was to feed the media frenzy that followed the *Apprentice* finale. Like it or not, next to Donald Trump I was the star attraction, and I don't think I was fully prepared for all the attention. I went on tour for about a week and a half, crisscrossing the country, promoting the show and Mr. Trump in such a relentless, nonstop way that I began to forget which points I had already made to which interviewer. It was exciting and new and all those good things, but it was also strange. It's disconcerting to have to respond intelligently every time someone sticks a microphone in your face, especially when there's a microphone in your face all day long. I warmed to the task soon enough, and by the end of the tour I was like a seasoned veteran. I began to understand what it must be like to move about in Mr. Trump's designer Italian shoes, the focus of such constant media attention, and to realize that this kind of high profile played a central role in his success. This wasn't what I'd expected, but it was now a part of my job and I welcomed the challenge to do it well. (And I quickly learned how to have a great time doing it.)

Ostensibly, I was hired as president of the Trump International Tower development project, but the reality was that I'd have several key people working very closely with me every step of the way. After all, I was hired as an apprentice. I took the designation very much to heart and reminded myself that Donald Trump didn't get where he was by handing over the reins of his business operations to inexperienced candidates—no matter how industrious or ambitious or promising they came across in interviews or on unscripted dramas played out over a period of several weeks before a prime time television audience. Mr. Trump is a show-me kind of guy, and I'd yet to show him a thing beyond my ability to outperform the fifteen other candidates on his show. The skills I put to work in order to survive his challenges and his boardroom interrogations would undoubtedly come into play on the construction site, but they were in no way an indication that I could manage such a massive project on my own.

All I knew was what I could expect of myself: to learn something new every day, to never make the same mistake twice, to surround myself with talented, experienced people and to make full use of their talents and experience, to soak in absolutely everything and become the professional sponge I wrote about earlier, and to confirm Mr. Trump's faith in me. If I had to accomplish these things with a set of training wheels for support and balance, that was fine by me . . . as long as they got accomplished.

As soon as the post-finale noise died down somewhat, I had some meetings with the in-house executive team that handles all real estate development for the Trump Organization. We met first in New York and then flew together to Toronto, where there was another high-rise project under way, and I went into these sessions with some concern. Not a whole lot of concern, mind you, but some, because these were to be the first meetings I'd have with members of Mr. Trump's team without Mr. Trump at my side.

Normally I'm a pretty confident guy going into any kind of new situation. I do my homework. I ask a lot of questions. Or, depending on the situation, I might hang back until I have something to contribute. Plus, I take a flexible approach to every business situation. Agility is essential if you mean to make it in any setting, and here I had to constantly shift my focus as my role reinvented itself from one day to the next.

Coming to this job in such a public, circus-like way, I worried that Mr. Trump's real estate executives wouldn't take me seriously if I came out firing questions and making studious notes. That's about the last thing you want when you're getting to know your new colleagues. If these guys wrote me off right out of the gate as some incompetent rookie, I'd never get anywhere. For all I knew, they already had me pegged as some green kid in over his head and resented the fact that they had to work with me, just so their boss could make even more of a name for himself on NBC. I didn't want to make a potentially difficult situation even worse.

> Take stock of a new situation before committing yourself to a new course of action.

I did a lot of listening during this first round of meetings. I stood off to the side and watched them do their thing on the Toronto job site, making mental note of how they dealt with the construction team there and how they presented themselves on behalf of Mr. Trump. I took the approach that I was there to learn, and figured these good people would come to respect that. If I came at them fast and furious with all kinds of questions, they'd likely dismiss me as some sort of neophyte, and if I took any kind of charge of these meetings they'd wonder who the hell I thought I was, so I played it mostly cool.

In retrospect, I don't think I needed to be so tentative about seeking out information, although in my defense I worried that I was in some ways foisted on these real estate development guys. They didn't hire me from a talented pool of applicants. They didn't put me through the paces and like how I came out on the other side. They didn't know me from a hole in one of their retaining walls. I was assigned to them, is all, and for all I knew, they might have thought they could have made a better hire drawing a name from a hat. They were stuck with me on the boss's say-so, and I was sensitive to that fact and careful not to give them any reason to question my qualifications. So what I did, under this small piece of uncertainty, was mostly keep quiet, even though it wasn't quite like me to keep quiet about anything. It's almost always okay to pepper your bosses and colleagues with questions, particularly if you find yourself in unfamiliar territory. Frequently they're the ones who brought you on board, so it's in their best interests to bring you up to speed, but just as frequently they'll need your input and expertise to keep them looking good and to keep the project on track.

Absolutely, you have to be an investigator whenever you're going into a new professional situation. You have to ask questions, do your homework, reach conclusions before they're presented to you as done deals. I hate to keep going back to the issue of MBA versus practical experience, but I truly believe that a good project manager earns his master's degree every time he or she tackles a new project—on a need-to-know basis. Textbook theory isn't always relevant, but practical experience and a thorough working knowledge of the business at hand are key. More than that, a healthy partnership will allow for all kinds of sharing of information, role-modeling, and mentoring.

A good leader knows when he's outgunned and needs to go back and gather reinforcements. That's the situation I found myself in. I needed help and I needed to learn as much as I possibly could as quickly as possible.

Most times, you have to grab help where you can find it, but sometimes you're lucky enough to find it at the top. One of the great things about working for The Trump Organization is that virtually every door is open to you. What this meant for me, early on, was virtually open-door access to one of most successful general contractors in real estate— Greg Cuneo, whose HRH Construction is one of the biggest firms in the country, with about $500 million in annual revenue. About fifteen years ago, Mr. Trump helped to launch Greg in business with a $50,000 "wedding gift," and here Greg has been only too happy to return the favor, letting me be a fly on the wall as he attends to details at the new Trump Place development on the Upper West Side of Manhattan and at other HRH projects around the city.

My association with Greg and his HRH team has been a true and vital apprenticeship during these first months; I have been allowed to learn every aspect of the development business, from reading construction drawings to trafficking supply orders to overseeing work crews. Three or four days a week for three or four hours at a stretch, Greg taught me theory, and he let me watch him turn that theory into practice. (About the best lesson I learned during these early tutorials was to be a hands-on presence at the job site; your team has got to see you and sense you over their shoulders if you expect to get results.)

If you don't know something, ask.

I didn't think of it as a publicity stunt or false advertising, me taking on this project. I actually saw myself running the entire construction operation—albeit with some considerable help. The Trump real estate team would be watching my back, and Mr. Trump himself intended to look over my shoulder for the first while. I welcomed his input, because the apprenticeship he has offered reaches beyond the nuts and bolts of this one building project. It's an apprenticeship in life, in moving about at these higher levels of big business. It's in learning how to promote yourself and your efforts in order to maximize your exposure and therefore your return. It's working alongside all these movers and shakers, and dealing with them on a kind of equal footing. And it's about tailoring your approach to the job at hand. With Cigars Around the World, for example, it made sense to maintain a loose, casual workplace environment— that side-by-side management technique I wrote about earlier. But here, with a monumental budget and a workforce to match, I'm guessing more of a top-down approach will be in order, and I'll look to Mr. Trump and his management team for pointers.

In the months since I've hired on, I've come to realize that there are parallels to this type of situation across corporate America. Every time a company brings in a new CEO to shake things up, particularly if it's someone from outside the industry, a learning curve gets factored into the equation. There's a certain amount of getting your feet wet, on both sides of the conference table. Some CEOs come in and clean house right away, which to me seems a fool move because you haven't had a chance to take the full measure of a situation. Others are content to ride out the current way of doing business, with the current team, to see where things go and where they might need some redirection. Each approach seems to suggest a certain style; the leader who wields the axe early might be more comfortable surrounding himself with his own hires, while the leader who adopts a wait-and-see approach might be keeping the old guard in place simply to have a place to point his finger if things fall apart.

In this situation, there were already plans in place long before I signed on to the project. There was a corps of architects, and a team of residential and retail salespeople. A lot of the construction work had already been awarded, and there were bids out on other aspects of the project as well. Things had been moving along at full tilt, and now that I was on board, it fell to me to define my role. As I looked ahead I saw that my principal responsibilities would be to work through my own corporate "punch list" and see that every eventuality was covered. That was one task I knew I could break down and do well, even with my relative inexperience. Someone's got to oversee the deliveries, the shift in market prices that might require a shift from steel to concrete in certain aspects of construction, and the distinctive design elements in our residential units. Someone's got to troubleshoot problems with the crew, run interference with the city, or smooth things over with neighbors who might not want a ninety-story high-rise in their backyards. I could be that all-important daily presence on the site to ensure that each piece of this intricate puzzle fit neatly alongside each other piece.

There's no denying the vast scope of this Chicago high-rise project, and one of the ways I got my mind around it was to look back on ancient Egyptian history and consider the construction of the Great Pyramids in contemporary development terms. It's astonishing, really, that these awesome monuments were ever built at all. At that time, only crude resources were available: handheld tools and nothing in the way of equipment and machinery beyond ropes and levers and pulleys. And yet somehow, these great mathematical and organizational minds were able to complete a workable design, assign a project manager to the task, parcel out areas of responsibility to other noblemen and craftsmen, and deploy thousands upon thousands of slaves to provide the energy to get the job done. It was the perfect marriage of design and execution, spun entirely from imagination and manpower. Even today, scholars scratch their heads in wonder at these colossal achievements, and as I caught a documentary on the History Channel one evening, I found myself doing the same.

Nothing is impossible.

The more I thought about it, the more I realized that the pyramids were built in much the same way you build a high-rise building. From a set of plans and a simple strategy. With a budget and on a timetable. One stone at a time. Then, as now, the same basic principles apply. Of course, slavery and the penalty of death are powerful motivational tools unavailable to today's project managers. (Even Donald Trump has his limitations!) But fear alone would not have been enough without the design and execution. The pyramids might have been built on the backs of tens of thousands of slaves, working under awful conditions, but the entire operation flowed from the design—from the power of one man to think the unthinkable and the power of many to see it through.

It was a humbling thing, to place this high-rise tower in this context, and as I did so, I realized that this next phase in my career was doable. I went from thinking it was beyond my reach to believing it was within my abilities. Because, in fact, building the Great Pyramids was a whole lot like building a ninety-story tower, which in turn is a whole lot building a career. You start with your plans, and then you do your homework and get all your paperwork and permits and financing in order. Next you pour the concrete and the forms to establish the building's footprint, and when that's taken care of, you pound these giant pylons into the ground to shore everything up. All of this takes time, but each step is straightforward, and at the other end you have your foundation and you can start in on construction. In New York, the convention is to build a deck in two days; in Chicago, it's a three-day deck process. Every three days, boom, another deck goes up, and three days later there's another deck on top of that one, on and on until you frame out the entire building. The higher you climb, the easier it gets, and soon enough you'll look up and see all ninety stories, all framed out and good to go. All along, underneath, there are crews following you up the ladder, completing the guts of the work, making sure the plumbing is stacked correctly and the ventilation is where it's supposed to be and the wiring is sound.

Everyone moving skyward, ever higher, until the work is complete.

And it all grows from the foundation. That's the toughest part of any job, and yet too often that's the piece some people want to race through. As I set these thoughts to paper now, I'm liking the metaphor and the message. Yes, the foundation is where it all starts—and if it doesn't start right, that's where it all ends. I look back over my own career to validate the point. If I hadn't recognized the value in opportunity when I started buying and selling cars back in high school, I'd still have that first Audi Fox sitting up on blocks in my mother's driveway. If my partner John and I hadn't had have the creativity and tenacity to get Cigars Around the World off the ground on our nothing budget, that business would have gone nowhere. If I hadn't had a spirit guide like Stuart Miller to help me lay in the groundwork on the very first residential properties I sought to redevelop, I could never have created the value that allowed me to turn those buildings around. And if I hadn't thrown my name in on the *Apprentice* audition or conducted myself with the integrity, resourcefulness, and agility it took a lifetime to develop, I would have never met Donald Trump or gotten the chance of that lifetime to work at his side.

There's a cliché in the real estate business which suggests that the true key to success can be reduced to three simple words: *location, location, location.* But I beg to differ—or at least to offer an alternative view. What it comes down to, really, is *foundation, foundation, foundation.* That applies not just to real estate but to any business endeavor. It applies to anything and everything we do, in business and in life. I was looking to establish a solid underpinning for the Trump International Tower *and* for a long, fruitful association with Donald Trump.

The plan, of course, is to build a great building in the greatest city in the world, and to get it done on time and under budget and to my boss's satisfaction. But beyond that, it's also to learn as much as I can, from as many different people as I can, as quickly as I can. Right now, it's just a twelve-month deal. That's what we were all playing for on the show—a one-year job at a salary of $250,000. But I didn't switch gears in the middle of a successful career just for the chance at a twelve-month gig. And I don't think Mr. Trump is looking on this as a short-term association, either. We've never talked about it, but he doesn't strike me as the kind of guy to go to all this trouble to make a token hire. If that was the case, why would he put me on a long-term project? And why would he be investing so much of his time to ensure my success? On paper, yeah, I'm on a one-year contract, but I'm looking on it as an open-ended deal. To think of it as anything less than a long-term association would be to sell myself short and to shortchange the good people who have placed their trust in me. I mean to see this project through, and I intend for it to work out well for me personally and for The Trump Organization. If it leads to bigger and better things with the company, that'd be great. If it takes me to where I can someday be doing deals *with* Donald Trump instead of *for* Donald Trump, that'd be great, too. And why not? He's always looking to expand his business, always in search of the next opportunity, and I can certainly imagine a scenario where we'd go partners on a building on Chicago.

> Promote your business. Promote your strategy. Promote your brand. Promote yourself.

I'll earn my stripes in my apprenticeship and one day stumble across a great piece of property and set up a meeting and say, "Hey, take a look at this deal."

Look, when Lebron James jumped straight from high school to the NBA, nobody expected him to match the big boys stride for stride, play for play—certainly not right away. Folks built some time into their expectations. As it turned out, he didn't need much time. He was ready to play at that level from the opening tip of his very first game. Me, I might need to log a season or two to get to the next level, but ultimately that's my goal. I plan on working until the day I die. I love to work. I live for it, really. In twenty years, I may not be developing real estate or selling cigars, but I'll be doing *something*. Something creative. Something entrepreneurial. Something that makes sense. And whatever I'm doing, there'll be a common thread from this opportunity with the Trump Organization to whatever comes next.

The lessons I'm learning from Donald Trump—cover every contingency, seize every opportunity, seek every advantage—go hand in hand with the lessons I learned from my father, and at the end of the day they're all about keeping your options open and taking full advantage. My father was only sixty-six years old when he died, and he was a *young* sixty-six. He had just retired, just bought himself a nice car, just started to treat himself to some of the finer things the world had to offer. He'd worked his whole life to take care of his family and was finally looking ahead to where he could take some time for himself. He was hoping to travel, to ski ... to *live* fully and without constraint, all of which only partly explains why his dying was such a raw deal. He was cheated out of so much that it pushed me to make a promise to myself: I will not be cheated. I don't think he would have felt cheated, but I certainly feel cheated on his behalf. And I'll make double-sure no one is left feeling cheated for my sake when my time is through. If I die tomorrow, so be it, but I'll check out knowing I've experienced a lot—and this roller-coaster ride with *The Apprentice* and Donald Trump will have everything to do with those experiences. I will soak in as much as I can from as many different people as I can, in whatever ways I can manage. I'll travel the world. I'll roll the dice. I'll try new things. At work and at play. Already I've learned how to sky-dive. I've learned how to snowboard. I'm planning to get my pilot's license. And on and on.

Keep open or stay closed, I keep reminding myself, because in my book, success comes down not only to meeting the challenges we set for ourselves but in thinking to set them in the first place.

Lessons Learned
ON SUCCESS

THINK THINGS THROUGH In a corporate environment, he who vacillates is toast. Be certain of your decisions and the paths you'll choose to implement those decisions. The cover-your-butt mentality that permeates virtually every office kills initiative, drive, and creativity. And it kills the true spirit of enterprise. But you do you want to maintain a defensible position in all that you undertake. I don't see a conflict in these two statements, although I'm guessing others might. Here's my take: A good idea, well executed, will always be a good idea, well executed, even if it results in a disappointing outcome. A bad idea, poorly executed, will be that disappointing outcome waiting to happen.

TAKE INVENTORY In order to run a successful business, you must inventory your assets on a regular basis. The same goes for running a successful career. Assess your personal assets and put them to maximum use. Are you a self-starter? An analytical thinker? A strong motivator? A relentless salesperson? Most people run down their list of skills and abilities and come up short. This is not a good thing. Next they tie their expectations to their shortcomings. Also, not a good thing. The top performer never says, "I'm not sure I can do this." It's not in his or her vocabulary. Instead, top performers flip the question. "Show me the walls," they'll say, "and I'll hurdle them."

FIT YOURSELF IN It's as tough to work alongside an arrogant MBA on the assembly line as it is to make room for the street-savvy upstart in the boardroom. If you let yourself be defined as any one type, you'll cut off opportunity. Understand your role. Are you there to offer support or to make things happen? Are you the go-to foot soldier or the big-picture executive? Know where and how and why you fit, and that it's the one-channel worker who gets slotted into one role. Be multichanneled.

UNDERSTAND YOUR CORE PURPOSE Why are you doing this? What are you hoping to accomplish? Where is your personal finish line? And what do you plan to do once you cross it? We chase our paychecks for different reasons, and it's important to recognize your end of the deal.

DRAW A PERSONAL BUILDING PLAN Have some idea what you've built, what you're building still, and what buildings you might like to see on the compound in years to come. And if you're lucky enough to be in a position to help other members of your family, be a good steward of your hard-earned resources. There's a wonderful phrase, "shirtsleeves to shirtsleeves," which has been used to describe the plight of the traditional family business in this land of immigrants, from one generation to the next. We start poor, working with our hands, in shirtsleeves. We achieve some measure of success and begin to drift from the work ethic upon which that success was built. We become seduced by the finer things in life. We squander what we've earned and return to working with our hands, in shirtsleeves. Know what you've built so that future generations can dwell within.

BALANCE (AGAIN!) As you can no doubt tell if you've read this far in these pages, I'm big on balance. It's at the root of everything I do. In fact, it's impossible to measure success in one aspect of your life without weighing it alongside the successes you've achieved in every other aspect of your life.

GIVE SOMETHING BACK Always. And give as much as you can. Also, always. Give of your time. For years, I've been volunteering at the Mercy Home for Boys in Chicago, and lately I've devoted myself to a youth scholarship my family has developed in my father's memory, and I mean to keep at it, no matter what fills my schedule in the days ahead, because it is only in the returning the favor that we can fully appreciate the favors that have been visited on us.

ACKNOWLEDGMENTS

I have been blessed with an amazing family that has been fiercely loyal through the years, in hard times and in great times, and for that I am truly thankful. My mother Gail has lived her life with tremendous courage and determination, and has always believed in me. I can't thank her enough. My sister Karen, who is also my assistant and one of my best friends, has been a constant with advice and support. My sisters Katie and Beth, who have always been there for me growing up and are still there for me today. To Sara, Rachel, Zak, Luke, Liam, Jacob, and Noah, who make being an uncle a fun job! And thanks to Mike Soenen, Craig Shannon, and Greg Pardue—three great brothers-in-law.

In business, as in life, many people don't know how good they have something until it is gone. I am fortunate to realize how good and true my friends have been, and I would like to pay tribute to them here. Jerry Agema, who has been like a brother to me for the past eighteen years. Adam Andrzejewski, my trusted friend and adviser, ever present with solid advice. Kyle Koch and Carson Sterling, always looking out for me. Chris Paustch, my good friend and computer expert, who has donated countless hours helping me set up websites. Zak Dich, who never lets me pay for a meal at his restaurant. Kathy Nakos, aka Ginger Salvatorie, for her quest for the good life. John Plummer, quick to lighten a tense moment with humor. A special thanks to Stuart Miller, a great friend. Illiana Romero, for cheering me on. Christine Collins and Kim Slotkus, two of my oldest friends. Thanks also to Mike

Acknowledgments

Palm, Ari Goldman, my friend and lawyer David Sachs, Jerry and Marcia Agema, Kevin Kickels, Sally Pullara, Rob Green, Scott Kozlowski—and Coach Ditka, for buying cigars from me in the early days when no one else would.

I cannot thank Donald Trump, Mark Burnett, and Conrad Riggs enough for taking a chance on an entrepreneur from Chicago. Jay Bienstock and Kevin Harris, for assembling an amazing production team: Bill Pruitt and Rob La Plante, along with Seth, Katherine, Jamie, Annelli, Sadoux, Patrick, Johnny, and the many other talented people who made *The Apprentice* happen. Thanks also to Carolyn and George, for their honest feedback in the boardroom. And a heartfelt nod to the fifteen other finalists from the show—true competitors all, who made me elevate my level of play.

Thanks to Jeff Zucker and his amazing team at NBC. To Jim Dowd, for opening my eyes to the media world. To Amanda Ruisi and Sean Martin, for all of their help. And to Carrie Simons, for her assistance on the West Coast.

I have to give credit to Dan Paisner, for his incredible ability to help me craft this book; to Josh Behar and his talented colleagues at HarperCollins, for working on such a tight deadline; and to Jennifer Rudolph Walsh, Jay Mandel, Mel Berger and the rest of the William Morris team, for guiding me in the right direction. Thanks also to Eric Seastrand, Brooke Slavik, and Betsy Berg—a great team to have on my side.

I am especially grateful to everyone at cigarsaround theworld.com and Synergy Brands. Jennifer Davenport, and Ben and Rick Torres, who have been with me since the beginning. Bryan Lafave, keep selling! And to Mair Fabish, Ernie Barbella, and Stephen Barbella at Synergy Brands, an extra special thanks for seeing the potential in me.